ARIEL WORKSHOP MANUAL

INCLUDES MAINTENANCE AND REPAIR DATA FOR ALL MODELS (1933-1951)

FOUR CYLINDER TWINS & SINGLES

ISBN: 1-58850-071-3
ORIGINALLY PUBLISHED BY FLOYD CLYMER IN 1965
THIS EDITION REPUBLISHED BY VELOCEPRESS IN 2007

COPYRIGHT 2007 VELOCE ENTERPRISES INC.,
SAN ANTONIO, TX 78230, USA.

INTRODUCTION

Welcome to the world of digital publishing ~ Using state of the art digital technology and equipment, **VelocePress** is able to bring titles back in print allowing you to access the information that you need, when you need it. Never has information been so accessible and it is our hope that this book serves your informational needs for years to come. While this edition is presented unchanged from the original 1952 edition, it has been reproduced using the latest print-on-demand technology.

If this is your first exposure to digital publishing, we hope that you are pleased with the results. Many more titles of interest to the classic automobile and motorcycle enthusiast are available via our website at **www.VelocePress.com**. We hope that you find this title as interesting as we do.

TRADEMARKS

INFORMATION ON THE USE OF THIS PUBLICATION

ARIEL MOTOR CYCLES

A PRACTICAL GUIDE COVERING
ALL MODELS FROM 1933

By

C. W. WALLER
Service Manager, Ariel Motors Ltd.

Published by
FLOYD CLYMER PUBLICATIONS
*World's Largest Publisher of Books Relating to
Automobile, Motorcycles, Motor Racing, and Americana*
222 NO. VIRGIL AVENUE, LOS ANGELES 4, CALIFORNIA

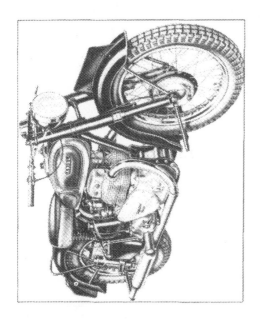

Ariel
Model 4G.
997 c.c. 4 Cyl.

Ariel
Model KH.
498 c.c. Twin.

ANNOUNCEMENT

We take pleasure in adding this U.S.A. Edition of the original *Ariel Motorcycle Owner's Handbook* to our ever-growing list of titles on automotive and motorcycle subjects. Compiled in England by a noted authority — Mr. C. W. Waller, service manager for Ariel Motors — this edition covers every phase in servicing all Ariel models, including the very newest machines.

We suggest that the section concerning the speed tuning of Red Hunter models will prove of special interest to the competition rider, and the comprehensive Index at the end of the book will certainly save the reader many minutes of "page thumbing".

Our chief reason for offering this book is, of course, because of the increased interest in British motorcycles in the U. S., and because reliable repair and maintenance data has been somewhat scarce. I am sure that every Ariel owner and enthusiast will find this manual of real value.

Floyd Clymer

Publisher

PREFACE TO THE THIRD EDITION

THE information contained in this book covers the maintenance and repair of the single-cylinder, twin-cylinder and four-cylinder Ariel machines produced between 1933 and 1951.

The "Square-Four" engine, fitted with an overhead camshaft, is dealt with in Chapter I, whilst the four-cylinder push-rod 600-c.c. and 1000-c.c. 1937-48 type engines and the 1949-51 "Square Four" light-alloy engine, are covered by Chapters II and III.

Chapter IV covers the engines for the twin-cylinder models, first introduced for the 1948 season.

Chapter V deals extensively with the single-cylinder engines, and a section at the end of the book has been devoted solely to the work of tuning the Red Hunter for competition work and trials.

Servicing of other components of the machine, such as wheels, hubs, brakes, etc., including the telescopic front fork fitted to all models beginning with 1947, will be found covered in various chapters.

Acknowledgments are due to *The Motor Cycle*, *Motor Cycling*, Messrs. Ariel Motors Ltd. and Joseph Lucas Ltd. for their permission to make use of certain illustrations in the book.

The publishers desire especially to thank Messrs. Ariel Motors Ltd. for permission to use the Ariel Trade Mark as a cover design, although the book is in no way a factory-sponsored production.

C. W. W.

CONTENTS

CHAP.   PAGE

I. 1933–1936 Square-Four Model (4F Engine)   9
    Oil Maintenance—Top Overhaul—Dismantling
    the Engine—Replacing Bearings—Checking Oil
    Pressure—Data Table.

II. 4/F/600-c.c. and 4/G/1000-c.c. Push-Rod
    Type Models (1937–1948).   .   .   .   15
    Maintenance of Lubrication System—Cleaning Oil
    Pump—Removing Cylinder Head and Rocker
    Box—Removing Rockers—Valve Removal—Valves
    and Seats—Engine Reassembly—Removing Cylin-
    der Block—Pistons—Gudgeon-pins and Bearings—
    Refitting the Cylinder Block—Crankcase and
    Crankshaft Dismantling—Crankshaft Assembly
    Gears—Timing Gear—Main Bearing—Connect-
    ing-rods—Camshaft Bearings—Valve Timing—
    Magneto Timing.

III. Model 4/G/1000-c.c. with Light-Alloy
     Engine (1949–1951).   39
     Construction—Maintenance of Lubricating Sys-
     tem—Distributor Unit—Decarbonisation—Remov-
     ing and Reassembling Cylinder Head—Dismantling
     Engine—Removal of Engine from Frame—Remov-
     ing Engine-shaft Shock Absorber—Removing
     Timing Gears—Removing Cylinder Block—
     Checking Main Bearings—Camshaft Bush and
     Bearing—Tappets and Guides—Ignition Timing—
     Technical Data.

IV. 500-c.c. Twin-Cylinder Models " KG " and
    " KH " (1948–1951).   59
    Construction—Lubrication—Valve Gear—Main-
    tenance—Lubrication System—Tappet Adjust-
    ment—Timing-chain Tensioner—Decarbonisation
    —Removing the Cylinder-head — Refitting the
    Cylinder-head—Dismantling Complete Engine—

Removing the Cylinder Block—Servicing Cylinder Bores—Removing Timing Gears and Chain—Removing Magneto and Dynamo—Engine Overhaul—Reassembling the Engine—Setting Valve Timing—Refitting Magneto and Dynamo—Setting Magneto Timing—Technical Data.

V.   SINGLE-CYLINDER ENGINE   83
Lubrication System — Oil-pressure Gauge — Air Leaks—Breather Valves—Timing Chain—Adjusting Tappets—Top Overhaul—Decarbonisation—Refitting and Adjustments—Crankcase Assembly Overhaul—Removal of Magdyno and Timing Gear—Cam Gear—Bearings—Ignition Timing—Data Tables.

VI.   GEARBOX AND CLUTCH ASSEMBLY .   .   .   113
Maintenance and Adjustments of the Clutch—Clutch Withdrawal Adjustment—Clutch Removal—Clutch Chain-wheel—Removing the Gearbox—Dismantling—Driving-gear Bushes—Reassembling—Foot Gear-change Mechanism—The Kick-starter—Speedometer Drive—Cork or Fabric Clutch—Data Table—Chain Adjustment.

VII.   CARBURETTER   129
" Amal " Carburetter—Adjustments and Tuning—Reconditioning—Air Leaks—Flooding—The " Solex " Carburetter—Air Strangler Type—Bi-starter Type—The Air Correction Jet.

VIII.   FRONT FORKS AND STEERING ASSEMBLY .   .   138
Girder Type Forks—Lubrication—Steering Head—Handlebar Mounting—Removal of Complete Steering Assembly—Removing Fork Girder—Dismantling Steering Damper—Fork Girder Repair—Front Fork Main Springs—Telescopic Front Forks—Maintenance—Auxiliary Coil Springs—Dismantling Telescopic Forks—Steering Damper—Data Table.

IX.   WHEELS, HUBS AND BRAKES   155
Front Wheel and Brake—Removal of Hub Ball Bearings—Rear Wheel and Brake with Fixed Wheel and Rigid Frame—Wheel Bearing Adjustment—Detachable Rear Wheel—Brake Adjustment—Wheel Alignment—Data Table.

CHAP.   PAGE

X. RIGID AND SPRING FRAMES 167

Rigid Frame—Head Races—Spring Frame—Dismantling Spring Frame Attachment—Reassembly —Data Table.

XI. THE RED HUNTER MODELS "VH" AND "NH" FOR COMPETITION USE 173

General Tuning of the Engine—Carburetter— Ignition—Lubrication—Control Cables—Gearbox —Silencers—Steering.

XII. ELECTRICAL EQUIPMENT 179

Lubrication—Contact Breakers—Lucas "Magdyno" Lighting Equipment—Contact Breaker Adjustment—Dynamo—Voltage Regulator—Electrical Service Notes and Test Data.

APPENDIX 196

Lubrication Recommendations.

INDEX 197

CHAPTER I

1933–1936 SQUARE-FOUR MODEL
(4F ENGINE)

THIS O.H.C. engine was first introduced in 1933, and is an exceptionally compact unit incorporating the well-known squared cylinder block and twin crankshafts. These shafts are mounted on fairly large single-journal ball bearings and are gear-coupled.

Routine adjustments are few, and consist mainly of rocker-arm adjustment for correct valve clearances, periodical checking of and setting the contact-breaker and sparking-plug points and attention to the carburetter.

Oil Maintenance

The 4F model was designed for long-distance, fast touring road work, and the engine runs very efficiently and maintains performance when so used. With frequent stopping and starting the engine has a tendency to set up internal condensation around the walls of the mag. and cam-chain covers. The water so formed drains into the crankcase sump and has a very adverse effect on the engine oil there. A "sludge" deposit builds up, and, although the oil filter is efficient, the quality of oil passed into the working parts of the engine soon impairs the life of ball bearings and piston-rings. It is, therefore, most essential frequently to flush out the crankcase and refill with clean oil if condensation is feared.

Maintenance of the carburetter and magdyno of the 4F model is similar to that of all other Ariel machines, and is dealt with in later chapters.

Top Overhaul

The simplicity of design of the 4F engine is such that the average rider can undertake the usual top overhaul without the use of special tools or fixtures, apart from the mag. and cam sprocket extractors which the makers provide in the tool-kit. A useful fixture, however, can be made up to assist with decarbonisation and valve removal after the cylinder head is removed, and this takes the form of a stout piece of board cut to the size of the underface of the cylinder head. On this board, four pieces of thick wood, shaped so as to fit into each separate combustion chamber, should be nailed or screwed. These blocks will press against the valve-heads and hold them hard against the seatings whilst the split valve cotters or cones are being removed. The valve-spring load is very light and they can be compressed with a small lever or screwdriver and the cotters will drop out. Rocker spindles can be withdrawn by screwing into each threaded end a $\frac{1}{4}$-in. $\times$ 26 T.P.I. bolt, pulling and slowly turning until all rockers and distance shims are free.

Decarbonisation is advisable every 3000–5000 miles.

Dismantling the Engine

If the more knowledgeable rider desires completely to dismantle the engine, this can first of all be removed as an entire unit from the frame without disturbing the petrol tank or gearbox. Here again no special tools are needed, but a useful fixture can be made up for assisting with the removal of the clutch housing. This is described in Chapter VI, dealing with the gearbox and clutch.

After removing the engine and dismantling the bottom half of the crankcase and the inner gear cover carrying the four big-end bearing dipper troughs, the crankshaft gear assembly can be lifted clear. Take note of the order of assembly, which is marked by centre punch dots on the coupling gears. The assembly is correct when the connecting-rods and pistons are diagonally opposed, *i.e.*, numbers one and three at top dead centre with numbers two and four at bottom dead centre and vice versa.

Replacing Bearings

To dismantle the crank assembly, which is necessary if the ball bearings are to be renewed, the assembly should be firmly fixed in a vice and a stout tube or box spanner used to remove the nuts securing the balance weights and flywheel disc to the shafts. The nuts are 1 in. across the flats of the hexagon, and are sunk into a recess formed in the balance weights, etc. It will be found necessary to grind away the outside diameter of the spanner to fit the nuts, and plenty of leverage should be applied to remove them; they are dead tight and right-hand thread. The gears and weights are keyed in position, and each assembly must be supported on a suitable fixture under a hand or power press in order to part the component pieces. Make a note of the order of assembly relative to the ball bearings slotted and standard, the slot to be fitted with the " H " shape locating piece in the crankcase housing. The refitting of the assembly and the complete unit is again carried out without any special apparatus. Reference should be made to the model 4F data sheet table (p. 12) in regard to the various settings.

Checking Oil Pressure

If oil pressure is low after having cleaned out the filter and pipe-lines, the trouble may lie with the ball valve situated immediately below the oil pump body. Access to this valve is made by removing the square slotted plug at the top of the groove in the side of the crankcase immediately below the timing-chain covers. Try reseating the steel ball after removing the coil spring, by inserting it into the end of a steel bar very lightly hollowed out and held in the seating by hand. One or two sharp taps on the end of the bar with a hammer will have the effect of forming a fresh seating in the soft pump body.

The crankcase oil level should never extend more than two-thirds up the flat on the dip stick, otherwise over-oiling of pistons, etc., will take place.

A useful data table is included with this chapter relative to sizes and fits of the most important components.

ARIEL MODEL 4/F/600-C.C. O.H.C.
1933–1936
DATA TABLE

Engine :

Capacity, actual	597 c.c.
Bore	56 mm.
Stroke	61 mm.
Compression Ratio	5·8–1
Peak revs.	6000
B.H.P.	24

Valve Timing :

Inlet Opens (before T.D.C.)	$\frac{1}{32}$ in. or 10°.
Inlet Closes (after B.D.C.)	$\frac{11}{32}$ in. or 50°.
Exhaust Opens (before B.D.C.)	$\frac{13}{32}$ in. or 55°.
Exhaust Closes (after T.D.C.)	$\frac{3}{64}$ in. or 15°.

Ignition Timing :

Before top dead centre, control fully advanced   5/16 in. max.

Valve Clearance :

(Adjustment to be carried out with engine cold.)

Inlet Valve	Nil.
Exhaust Valve	Nil.

Valve Head and Seating Angle . . . 45°

Contact Breaker Gap . 0·012 in.

Sparking-Plug Point Gap . 0·015 in.–0·018 in.

Piston-Ring Gap :
    Compression Rings . 0·006 in.–0·007 in.
    Oil Control Rings . 0·018 in.–0·020 in.

Piston Clearance in Cylinder Bore :
    Ring Land . . . 0·017 in.–0·019 in.
    Below Rings . . 0·006 in.–0·008 in.
    Extreme Skirt . . 0·004 in.–0·006 in.

Gudgeon-pin :
    Diameter . . . $\begin{cases} 0·624 \text{ in. or } \frac{5}{8} \text{ in. } -0·001 \text{ in.} \\ 0·6245 \text{ in. or } \frac{5}{8} \text{ in. } -0·0005 \text{ in.} \end{cases}$

S.E. Bush :
    Ream after fitting to . $\begin{cases} 0·625 \text{ in. or } \frac{5}{8} \text{ in. } +0·000 \text{ in.} \\ 0·6245 \text{ in. or } \frac{5}{8} \text{ in. } -0·0005 \text{ in.} \end{cases}$

Valve Stem—Inlet and Exhaust :
    Diameter . . . $\begin{cases} 0·280 \text{ in.} \\ 0·281 \text{ in.} \end{cases}$

Valve Guide—Inlet and Exhaust :
    Internal diameter . . $\begin{cases} 0·2815 \text{ in.} \\ 0·2825 \text{ in.} \end{cases}$

Half-Time Shaft Bush :
    Ream after fitting to . $\begin{cases} 0·750 \text{ in. or } \frac{3}{4} \text{ in. } +0·000 \text{ in.} \\ 0·7495 \text{ in. or } \frac{3}{4} \text{ in. } -0·0005 \text{ in.} \end{cases}$

B.E. Bearing Size :
    Roller type (Nos. 1, 2, 4) $\frac{25}{32}$ in. × 1·688 in. × 0·4175 in.
    (No. 3) . $\frac{15}{16}$ in. × 1·938 in. × 0·4175 in.

Oil Pressure : 15–20 lbs./sq. in.

Camshaft Ball Bearing Size :
    Drive End . . . $\frac{3}{4}$ in. × 1$\frac{7}{8}$ in. × $\frac{9}{16}$ in.
    Opposite End . . $\frac{5}{8}$ in. × 1$\frac{9}{16}$ in. × $\frac{7}{16}$ in.

Half-Time Shaft Ball Bearing :
    Size . . . . $\frac{3}{4}$ in. × 1$\frac{7}{8}$ in. × $\frac{9}{16}$ in.

Crankshaft Ball Bearing Size :
    Slotted Outer Race . 1$\frac{1}{8}$ in. × 2$\frac{1}{2}$ in. × $\frac{5}{8}$ in.
    Standard Plain Race . 1$\frac{1}{8}$ in. × 2$\frac{1}{2}$ in. × $\frac{5}{8}$ in.

Camshaft Chain . . $\frac{3}{8}$ in. × 62 Endless.

Magneto Chain	.	$\frac{3}{8}$ in. $\times$ 61 Endless.
Magdynamo . .	.	Lucas MNIE.
1932/5 . . .	.	Separate Distributor.
1936 . . .	.	Combined Unit Distributor
Carburetter . .	.	Amal.

Auxiliary Coil Springs.

Code : " Yellow Spot " .	.	Solo type.
Number of coils .	.	20
Wire gauge . .	.	0·202 in.
Code : " Red Spot "	.	Side-car type.
Number of coils .	.	19 + $\frac{1}{2}$.
Wire gauge . .	.	0·212 in.

FRAME INTERCHANGEABILITY (RIGID AND SPRING)

RIGID FRAME.

The single-cylinder rigid frame is interchangeable with every model 500-c.c., 350-c.c. and 250-c.c. produced in 1936 and subsequent, excepting the 1939 250-c.c. lightweight models. All engine and gearbox fixing plates, frame bolts, etc., are likewise identical.

SPRING FRAME (SINGLE-CYLINDER).

The spring frame, first manufactured in 1939, can be fitted to all models produced since 1936, excepting the 1939 lightweight 250-c.c. Engine plates, etc., are identical.

SPRING FRAME (FOUR-CYLINDER).

The spring frame (four-cylinder type) can be fitted only to the 1937–1951 Square Four 1000-c.c. and the 1939 four-cylinder 600-c.c. Engine plates, etc., are identical.

CHAPTER II

MODELS 4/F/600-C.C. and 4/G/1000-C.C. PUSH-ROD TYPE (1937–1948) WITH CAST-IRON CYLINDER BLOCK AND HEAD

THE model 4/F/600-c.c. was produced for the 1939 season only, and the makers do not intend to continue with this further. All maintenance and servicing remarks apply to both models, however, and the engine of the 600-c.c. is identical in layout except, of course, in regard to bore and stroke and size of cylinder head, valves and connecting-rods. The Solex Bi-Starter carburetter is fitted to the 1938–1948 1000-c.c. models, but not to the 1937 or the 600-c.c. type.

General maintenance of the engine is confined chiefly to adjustment of rockers, magneto and carburetter, cleaning out of the oil-tank, pipe-line and sump.

Maintaining the Lubrication System

To maintain the efficiency of the lubrication system (see Fig. 1) it is essential to ensure perfect cleanliness throughout. The oil-tank and crankcase sump should be drained every 1000 miles and the gauze filters thoroughly washed with petrol, as well as flushing out the tank and sump base. When replacing the crankcase filter make quite sure that the spring-loaded disc is placed uppermost.

Cleaning Oil Pump

The oil pump should be removed completely from the crankcase for cleaning purposes. The pump is situated in the timing gear case and driven by a small spindle extension formed on the camshaft gear nut. To remove the pump it is only necessary to release the two hexagon nuts and lock washers and gently prise off the fixed studs. Hold the pump between vice jaws, but cover the two

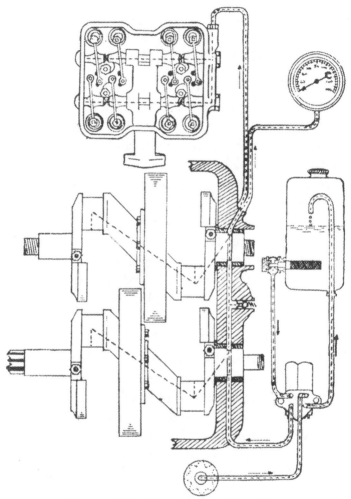

FIG. 1.—THE LUBRICATION SYSTEM.

Oil is drawn from the tank and passes through an oilway in the crankcase wall to the two main bearings and thence through the drilled crankshafts to the big-ends. A separate feed is taken to the rocker box and a connection made to the oil gauge. The oil drains down into the star-shaped filter in the sump and is then pumped back into the tank for further circulation.

faces with a small thin guard of wood or fibre to prevent damage.   Remove the pump base plugs or caps and expose the spring-loaded ball valves.   Thoroughly wash out and examine the pump plungers and ball seatings for any sign of scoring or foreign matter.

Before reassembling, place the steel balls on their respective seatings and with the aid of a short steel bar and hammer give each ball a sharp tap.   This has the effect of keeping the seating contours in relation to the balls.   Before replacing the small coil springs, lightly stretch them to increase tension.   Tighten both plugs securely and wipe the pump and crankcase pump faces and refit, but ensure that the pump washer is in good condition.

The duralumin sliding block operating the two pump plungers must be perfectly free in the guides, but should not be allowed to wear to excess, or loss of movement and undue noise will occur.   The oil-pressure valve should be occasionally removed and dismantled for cleaning, and the ball and spring treated in the same way as those of the oil pump.

DECARBONISATION

Removing Cylinder Head and Rocker Box

With a new engine recently run in, it is recommended that the cylinder head be removed for examination and cleaning after 2000–3000 miles.   After this, it is only necessary to repeat the operation every 5000–6000 miles to maintain maximum efficiency.

The order of procedure in removing the cylinder head complete with rocker box attached is a very simple one and does not require any special tools or fitments.   The petrol tank need not be removed.

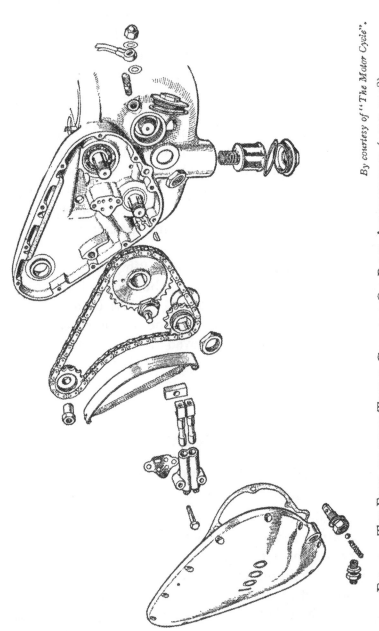

By courtesy of "The Motor Cycle".

FIG. 2.—THE FOUR-CYLINDER TIMING GEAR AND OIL PUMP ARRANGEMENT (1937–1948). The chain drives the camshaft and magdyno.   Showing also oil filter and relief valve in timing case cover.

After detaching the carburetter, exhaust pipes and rocker-box cover, the twelve securing bolts are removed, and it is advisable first to take out the four extended centre bolts which pass through the rocker box. These are the bolts which carry the four rocker-box cover dome nuts. Prise up the head just enough to allow the eight push-rods to clear the top of the cylinder block and withdraw them sideways.

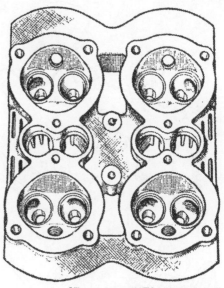

Support the head complete with rocker box and all fittings on the bench by placing it on two lengths of thick board strips to

[By courtesy of " The Motor Cycle".

FIG. 3.—THE FOUR-CYLINDER HEAD.

prevent the extended ends of the push-rods being damaged.

Removing Rockers

The rockers must be removed before attempting to dismantle further, and to do so the rocker spindles are withdrawn by detaching the hexagon cap nuts and pulling the spindles out by using one of the long centre head bolts, screwed $\frac{5}{16}$ in. × 26 T.P.I. into the exposed end of each spindle. Lay out, in correct order, on the bench all rockers, distance washers, steel shims and push-rods, taking note that shims are fitted only to prevent rockers directly touching the aluminium spindle bearings.

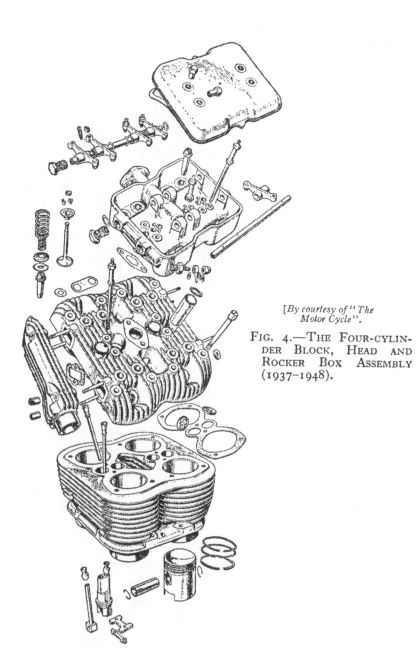

[By courtesy of "The
Motor Cycle".

FIG. 4.—THE FOUR-CYLIN-
DER BLOCK, HEAD AND
ROCKER BOX ASSEMBLY
(1937–1948).

Valve Removal

The makers supply a valve-spring compressor to facilitate spring removal, but the actual spring rate or load is very light and providing the valve heads are kept pressed into their seatings any simple improvised tool can be used. A useful fitment to make up for retaining the valves in position whilst compressing springs is described in Chapter I, dealing with the 1936 Square Four, consisting of a board and four suitable blocks. An old $\frac{1}{2}$-in. tube spanner, suitably slotted at one end, can be used to fit against the spring collar to compress the valve springs and the split cones or cotters will fall away.

Valves and Seats

Always examine the hardened valve-stem end caps for wear ; although these can be refaced, renewal is advisable if the pitting is deep. Each valve should be ground to its respective seating and not interchanged. Inlet valves are those with the stem undercut below the head and are the four inside ones numbered 2, 3, 6 and 7. Note that the large coil of the inner valve spring fits next the collar with taper hole. The usual method is employed when grinding in the valves, and here again no special tools are required.

Valve seatings should be examined for signs of pitting or " pocketing " and if it is found that a good ground angle cannot be obtained, the seating in the cylinder head should be lightly recut with a seating cutter tool of 45°, using a pilot stem clearance fit in the valve guide. It may be necessary, at some period during the life of a valve, to reface it with the aid of the workshop refacing machine, but these operations are best carried out by a competent mechanic only.

Ensuring a Clean Engine

If an oil leakage is suspected at the rocker-box and cylinder-head joint it is advisable at this stage to remove the box for examination and refacing if necessary. To remove the rocker box from the cylinder head, with all rockers and valves already dismantled, the two nuts screwed on the two centre studs in the centre of the underside of the head should be removed. This will release the induction joint between the cylinder head and rocker box. Next press or drive out, with a stepped or double-diameter drift punch, the valve guides, taking care to support the whole assembly firmly in the press or on the bench whilst operating. The rocker box is now parted from the head and should be thoroughly cleaned and very lightly refaced on a flat surface-plate, using a little very fine emery paste or cloth. Check valve guides for internal ovality wear and renew if this is excessive. Reference to the data chart at the end of this chapter should be made for sizes.

Reassembling

Refit the rocker box to head after placing new joint washers in position, but it is advisable to smear these with a little high-class jointing compound beforehand. Then refit and tighten up the two induction centre-stud nuts. Lightly coat the valve guides with compound and press into position with the shouldered portion inside the box. Reassemble all valves, rockers, push-rods, etc., not forgetting the eight valve end caps. If convenient leave the assembly of head and box after refitting to set overnight before running the engine, and thus ensure a perfect oil-tight joint. Make sure the cylinder-head gaskets, which are now of the copper and asbestos type, are in good condition and place on the cylinder block so that all bolt holes are in line. When replacing cylinder head to block take care to screw down each holding bolt in turn very little at a time until quite tight. After running the engine for a short period try tightening each bolt in turn again. Refer to the data chart again for valve clearances and to Chapters VII and XII referring to carburetter and magneto adjustments.

Removing Cylinder Block

During the process of decarbonisation, if it is desired to examine the pistons, the cylinder block can be removed by unscrewing the eight holding stud nuts and lifting the block clear. The two rear nuts situated between the magdyno and the cylinder block can be removed with a special spanner, made up from a length of hexagon steel bar and the cut-off end of an ordinary open-ended spanner welded on to one end of the bar at a right angle. The top of the hexagon can be turned with another spanner or wrench.

Pistons

To remove the pistons from the connecting-rods the circlips or lock rings must be prised out of their grooves with the pointed end of an old screwdriver or scribing tool. If the gudgeon-pins are at all tight for any reason, they can be lightly driven out by supporting one side of the piston and using as a drift or punch an old pin or bar of slightly smaller diameter. If the original pistons are to be refitted, mark them in correct order, numbers 1, 2, 3, 4 clockwise, commencing with right-hand front as number one.

The pistons and cylinder bores should be examined and checked for wear. Cylinder block should be re-newed or reground if bore wear exceeds 0·008 in., and pistons likewise renewed if bearing faces at the skirt have worn to increase the clearance 0·004 in. above standard.

Piston-rings should be replaced if the gaps exceed 0·030 in. when tested in their respective bores.

Gudgeon-pins and Bearings

The gudgeon-pins tested in the small-end bushes should not exceed 0·003 in. clearance. Small-end bushes can be removed with connecting-rods in position by using a form of draw bolt and bush made up from an old bush reduced slightly in diameter outside and pulled through the connecting-rod end by tightening the draw-bolt nut. New bushes can be inserted in the reverse way and hand

FIG. 5.—METHOD OF REPLACING CYLINDER BLOCK—1939
600-C.C. 4F MODELS

reamed after fitting. Refer to data chart *re* sizes and clearances. When fitting the pistons and gudgeon-pins it is advisable to renew all circlips owing to loss of tension during removal.

Refitting the Cylinder Block

This is best carried out with assistance, but if single-handed, the engine should be rotated slowly until all pistons are at the same level and two steel strips, 9 in. × 1 in. × $\frac{3}{32}$ in., for the 600-c.c., and wood strips, 9 in. × $\frac{1}{4}$ in. × $\frac{7}{16}$ in., for the 1000-c.c., placed across the top of the crank-case to support the four pistons in a vertical position whilst lowering the block. Ensure that all ring gaps are staggered in relation to each other and the block is lowered very carefully whilst compressing each ring in turn as it enters the respective bores. The rings and bores should be smeared with clean oil before fitting.

Crankcase and Crankshaft Dismantling

This is only necessary when crankshaft roller and plain and the big-end bearings require renewal. Heavy oil consumption, loss of pressure and bearing knock are symptoms that wear is present in these bearings. The engine can be removed as a complete unit from the cycle frame if so desired, and the first operation is to dismantle the primary chaincase, chain and clutch. Foot-rests also are removed, and after taking off the securing nut, the foot-rest should be given a sharp blow downwards with a hammer to loosen the taper fitting.

The Engine Shaft Shock Absorber is best dismantled with the engine still in the frame, and it is only necessary to release the tab or lock-washer between the two securing nuts and the assembly can be removed. For future reference the order of assembly is as follows: driving sprocket, sliding member, spring-retaining collar, spring, spring plate, hardened steel washer, locknut, tab washer and final locknut. This assembly is not adjustable, and locknuts are intended to be tightened to the fullest travel.

Drain and remove the oil-tank, battery and battery carrier. Remove the rear engine plates and withdraw the gearbox after detaching the rear chain. Support the engine by placing suitable packing under the crankcase, and then remove the front engine plates. The complete crankcase can then be withdrawn from the frame.

Crankcase Bearing Oil Seal

Due to wear of the driving-side crankcase roller bearings, it sometimes occurs that an excessive amount of oil enters the coupling gear housing and is subsequently

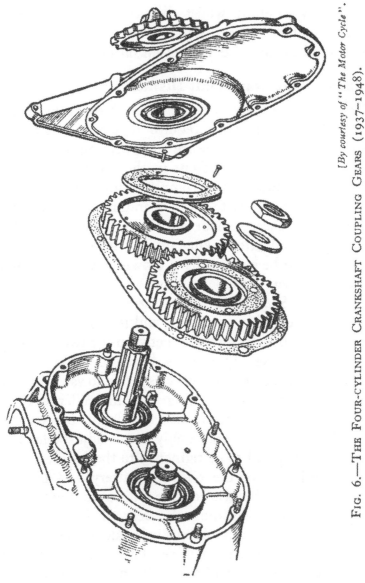

[By courtesy of "The Motor Cycle".

FIG. 6.—THE FOUR-CYLINDER CRANKSHAFT COUPLING GEARS (1937–1948).
The fibre discs on the gears prevent ring and the gear cover forms the back plate of the primary chain case.

forced through the outer bearing into the primary-chain case, causing a very high oil level and leakage into the clutch housing.

Without completely dismantling the engine to renew

roller bearings, a special self-adjusting oil-seal can very easily be fitted between the bearing in the gear cover and the rear coupling gear. The seal can be obtained direct from the makers' Service Dept. or from Ariel dealers, but it must be noted that this fitment is incorporated as standard on all 1948 models.

To fit, it will be necessary to remove the primary-chain cover and coupling-gear cover as illustrated in Fig. 6, and the seal is then placed over the splined driving shaft, but finally located on the extractor thread of the rear coupling gear.

Crankshaft Assembly Gears

Fix the assembly firmly on the bench and remove the crankshaft coupling-gear cover, taking care that the large roller bearing housed in same, and which has an inner race with a centre bore 0·001 in. smaller than those in the main crankcase, is marked for replacement in same order if not to be actually renewed. Remove the front crank-shaft nut securing the coupling gear and the gears are then ready for extraction. The makers can now supply a special set of crankshaft coupling-gear extractors, which also incorporate a fitment for reassembling the gears on each respective shaft. In the absence of the factory set large screw-type extractors, of the same design as those in the tool-kit for magneto sprocket removal, can be machined up if desired. Reference to the data table (pp. 36–38) will give gears and shaft thread sizes. The coupling gears are a press fit on the straight shafts, which also incorporate standard-type steel keys. Note that the teeth on each coupling gear are marked with centre dots in two places for correct meshing and either pair of such markings can be used, providing the single marked gear meshes between the opposite two marked gears.

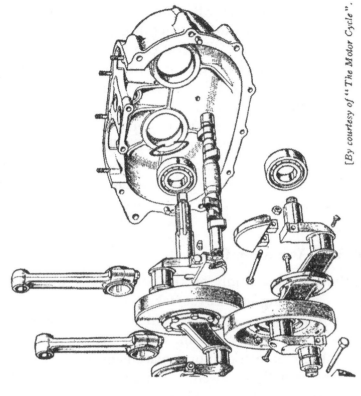

FIG. 8.—THE FOUR-CYLINDER CRANKSHAFT ASSEMBLY (1937–1948).

FIG. 7.—THE FOUR-CYLINDER TIMING SIDE CRANKCASE (1937–1948).

Showing crankshaft plain bearings and oil return from sump filter.

Important Note

When refitting the gears, care should be taken to ensure the correct register of the two keys in their respective keyways, otherwise incorrect alignment will result.

Timing Gear

Removal of the timing gear entails the extraction of the oil pump, as previously described, and the withdrawal of the magneto, camshaft, and crankshaft sprockets. The Weller tensioner blade should be held down to reduce pressure on the chain whilst removing the three sprockets; a strong paper clip can be adapted for this purpose. The camshaft sprocket nut is a left-hand thread. The mag. sprocket is a centre taper fit and the camshaft and crankshaft sprockets keyed and parallel. A steel oil-seal washer is fitted behind the rear crankshaft sprocket and front nut. Take note when reassembling to fit the camshaft sprocket with the raised centre boss inwards. Remove the magdyno from the platform after removal of the hexagon fixing bolt underneath and the top securing strap. Lift the magdyno

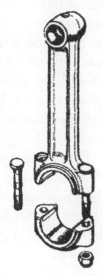

FIG. 9.—CON- NECTING - ROD FITTED WITH PLAIN WHITE- METAL BEARINGS (1937–1947).

to clear the base dowels and note the special joint rubber washer between the crankcase and the magneto end cover.

Checking the Main Bearing

After removing the screwed cap which plugs the timing side main front bearing, the crankshaft nut and oil-seal washer can be detached. After *all* crankcase bolts securing the two halves have been removed the crankcase can be parted and the camshaft and crankshaft assembly withdrawn.   The timing side plain crankshaft bearings should be examined for wear and score marks, and if a clearance exceeding 0·004 in.–0·005 in. is found the bearings should be replaced.   To remove, gently warm up the crankcase surrounding the bearings, remove the grub screws or securing set pins and press out with a suitable mandrel or press tool.   The bearing bushes, which are white-metal lined, must be pressed into the interior of the half crankcase.   New bushes supplied by the makers require to be re-bored after being pressed in owing to certain contraction, and a finished clearance of 0·001 in.–0·0015 in. should be allowed for crankshaft fit.   Location of the oilways must be watched to ensure the oil-feed holes being in line with the corresponding oil feed in the crankcase.

Excepting 1948 engine units, which are not fitted with securing pins or grub screws, when new bushes are fitted they will require drilling $\frac{13}{64}$ in. $\times$ $\frac{1}{8}$ in. deep to receive the pin or screw, but care must be taken not to exceed the depth of $\frac{1}{8}$ in., otherwise the white-metal lining may be pierced.

Connecting-rods (1937-1947 Models only)

The connecting-rods, which are of Hiduminium light alloy, have a split plain white-metal big-end bearing. Very little bearing wear takes place under 20,000 to 30,000 miles, and remetalling should not be really necessary before this, unless through a failure with the lubrication system or some defect in the metal lining appearing. The white metal is 0·020 in. in thickness and is applied direct to the connecting-rod.   Serviced connecting-rods should be fit-tested to the crank journal and very lightly scraped until a drag is felt when bolted up securely.   The alloy rod expands under running temperatures and with the presence of hot oil will therefore lose the above-mentioned drag after a few minutes' running. Care should be taken to ensure the big-end bearing bolts being fitted right home and with firmly cottered nuts.

Connecting-rods (1948 Models)

Certain series of engines during 1948 were fitted with a modified type of rod incorporating a big-end bearing consisting of two separate loose shell liners, white metalled. The liners are supplied in pairs when replacements are needed, and as they are all finished to determined standard size no special instructions are necessary relative to fitting, other than to ensure that location is correct when the rod is assembled to the crank journal.

The original slotted-type big-end bearing securing nuts' have been replaced with Simmonds Pinnacle locknuts which do not need cotter pins. It is permissible to use these nuts again after removal, but for security reasons it is really advisable to replace the full set.

No attempt should be made to fit the 1948 separate-shell-type liners to the 1937–47 original white-metalled-type connecting-rods, but a set of the 1948 rods complete with loose liners can be fitted to the early pattern crankshaft assembly. If this is done it will be found necessary to grind deeper chamfers on the balance weights to permit the thicker rod end caps to clear when rotated.

The 1948 connecting-rod is fitted with the Simmonds B.E. nuts uppermost, and therefore it is possible to remove the nuts, bolts and bottom bearing caps with the crankcases in position in the frame of the cycle. To replace a big-end bearing (loose liners), it is only necessary to remove the cylinder block and expose all B.E. bearing nuts, etc. To prevent the nuts, bolts, etc., from dropping into the crankcase, it is advisable to place a cloth beneath each rod before dismantling.

Be Sure to Clear Oilways

Before refitting the connecting-rods it is advisable to thoroughly clear out the crankshaft drilled oilways. Remove the screwed small plugs in each crankshaft, with a length of stiff wire scrape out all deposits of foreign matter and wash out with clean petrol. See that the big-end oil-feed hole in each crank journal is perfectly clear, and test with a $\frac{3}{32}$-in. drill.

Inspect the Crankcase and—

With the crankcase now dismantled, the timing-side half can be examined for any signs of a crack or fracture at the very important flange surrounding the magneto sprocket hole. This flange acts as an oil-path or narrow trough, and all excess oil thrown up and around the magneto sprocket is drained away from the hole, where otherwise it would have a tendency to enter the armature housing. A broken flange can and should be patched by aluminium welding and cutting or filing a new groove. The coarse return or reverse thread on the back of the mag. sprocket should just clear the hole in the crankcase, and the sprocket must be as near perfect centre as possible.

—the Timing Chain

Examine the pivot ends of the Weller tensioner blade and spring hooks, and if at all worn, renewal is advisable.

A worn timing-chain fibre rubbing strip will create undue noise, especially at slow engine speeds. To remove the strip, the three securing rivets must be drilled countersunk and punched out. New rivets with the head well up in the fibre-strip must be firmly supported when riveting the ends into the aluminium crankcase flange. Rapid fibre-strip wear is usually attributed to a worn timing chain or tensioner. Driving-side crankcase roller bearings have their outer lipped races pressed into the crankcase and held by circlips. The race housing is parallel bored. The lipped side of the race is located next to the circlip groove. Worn or pitted roller bearings should be replaced, and, when pressing in or out, slightly warm the crankcase housing to avoid scoring and subsequent slackness.

Camshaft Bearings

The camshaft bush located in the drive-side crankcase when requiring replacement can be withdrawn from the blind housing by warming the surrounding metal and inserting a tight-fitting reamer, which, when slowly turned and pulled, will extract the bush.

The new bush must be drilled after fitting to correspond with the oil-feed hole in the housing.

Reassembling

When reassembling the crankshafts and crankcases make quite sure that all joint faces are clean and a smear of good jointing compound applied.

Do not omit to fit the oil-seal " steel thick plain " washers behind the crankshaft sprocket and the front shaft nut. When coupling gears and chain sprockets have been refitted the magneto and camshaft timing must be correctly set according to the data chart (see page 36).

Valve Timing

Generally, it will be found that when the two holes on the camshaft sprocket are pointing downwards and in line with the timing mark on the crankshaft sprocket with No. 1. piston at T.D.C., correct valve timing will result.

The above method, however, cannot always be guaranteed to give an accurate 100 per cent. setting, and with certain series of engines it is not possible to follow the markings at all. The maker's service mechanics always set valve timing by the original method of inserting a fine-reading steel rule in the plug orifice of No. 1. cylinder and setting the piston at $\frac{3}{16}$ in. before T.D.C. This operation should be carried out before finally fitting the crankshaft sprocket and chain.

With the piston correctly set, the camshaft should be turned by lightly positioning the sprocket until the inlet valve just commences to open. This is best determined by setting the valve-stem clearance at 0·002 in. only and sliding the rocker arm across the face of the valve end cap until " lift " is felt.

After obtaining the correct setting of No. 1. inlet valve, it is then essential to offer up the small crankshaft sprocket on one of the three keyways provided and test the timing chain for easy meshing. This is a trial-and-error operation and may entail trying all three key positions before the chain locates without " riding " sprocket teeth.

When sprockets are fixed and tightened, adjust valve clearances to correct data setting, and as No. 1. cylinder timing is now correct, Nos. 2, 3 and 4 will automatically follow through using an integral one-piece camshaft.

Magneto Timing

The ignition timing is set after bolting the magdyno in position, and the most convenient cylinder to work on is No. 1 or right-hand front. Setting the piston at $\frac{5}{16}$ in. (1000-c.c.) and $\frac{3}{16}$ in. (600-c.c.) before T.D.C. of the compression stroke with both valves closed will be correct with the control in the fully advanced position and the breaker points just opening. At this setting the magneto sprocket, with the chain already in position over same, as well as over the camshaft and crank sprockets, should be tapped on with a box or tube spanner placed over the spindle. Finally, check the timing and tighten the armature nut.

Timing the Distributor

This is best carried out by checking on No. 1 cylinder as for the magneto timing and the settings of $\frac{3}{16}$ in. for the 600-c.c. and $\frac{5}{16}$ in. B.T.D.C. for the 1000-c.c. are the same for setting the rotor arm. The timing-indicator line on the rotor segment or blade should correspond with the line on the aluminium base-plate of the distributor cover when all backlash has been taken up by turning the rotor by hand anti-clockwise. To alter the position of the rotor, this should be gently pulled off the steel adaptor carrying it, and the small centre fixing screw removed. The adaptor can then be prised upwards and reset in the desired position. The distributor spiral gears are driven by the dynamo gear by way of a separate detachable driving-dog. If the dynamo is ever removed for cleaning or adjustment, take care not to turn the engine, otherwise the magneto rotor timing will be altered.

To remove the vertical spiral distributor gear it is necessary first to unscrew the complete greaser, as the threaded shank of this acts as a safe location for the gear.

Check the distributor cover for cracks or "tracking" (H.T. short circuit) and, when the engine and oil-tank are refitted into the frame, take care to ensure that the main H.T. cable from pick-up to distributor is not pinched between the tank, or H.T. leakage will occur at this point if ordinary rubber cable is used.

No special instructions are necessary for refitting the engine and gearbox into the frame, except to always loosely assemble the rear engine plates and gearbox in position first, finally positioning the front plates and tightening very securely all fixing bolts and nuts.

Note the order of firing is Nos. 1, 2, 3 and 4.

After running the engine for a short period with the rocker cover removed, check the oil pipe-line to rocker box to ensure that it is clear and oil is flowing through the hollow rocker spindles.

In wet weather, water is liable to flow on to the distributor cover and cause a short circuit in the system, with subsequent misfiring. A suitable cover for the distributor can be made up with a piece of oiled silk or similar material and extended over the H.T. leads under the petrol tank. Good quality waterproofed and heavily insulated cables can be substituted for the soft rubber type supplied by the makers, with very lasting benefits.

Data Table

1937–1948 1000-C.C. MODEL 4G AND 1939 600-C.C. MODEL 4F
(With Cast-Iron Cylinder Block and Head)

	Bore.	Stroke.	Capacity, Actual.	B.H.P.	Peak Revs.	Compression Ratio.
Engine :						
(4F) 600-c.c.	mm.	mm.	c.c.			
model .	50·4	75	599	23	5600	6·9–1
(4G) 1000-						
c.c. model	65	75	997	36	5800	5·8–1

Valve Timing :

Inlet Valve Opens (before T.D.C.) . . .	$\frac{3}{16}$ in. or 25°.
Inlet Valve Closes (after B.D.C.) . . .	$\frac{1}{2}$ in. or 55°.
Exhaust Valve Opens (before B.D.C.) .	$\frac{19}{32}$ in. or 60°.
Exhaust Valve Closes (after T.D.C.) . .	$\frac{1}{8}$ in. or 20°.

Ignition Timing :

(Before top dead centre, control fully advanced.)	1000-c.c.	$\frac{6}{16}$ in.
	600-c.c.	$\frac{3}{16}$ in.

Valve Clearance :

(With engine cold.)

Inlet Valve .	.	0·006 in.
Exhaust Valve .	.	0·008 in.

Piston-ring Gap . . 0·010 in.–0·012 in.

Piston Clearance in Cylinder Bore :

Ring Land . . .	1000-c.c.	0·016 in.–0·019 in.
	600-c.c.	0·017 in.–0·019 in.
Below Rings . .	1000-c.c.	0·004 in.–0·006 in.
	600-c.c.	0·003 in.–0·005 in.
Extreme Skirt . .	1000-c.c.	0·002 in.–0·004 in.
	600-c.c.	0·002 in.–0·004 in.

Oil Pressure (Adjustable) : . approx. 40 lb. per sq. in.

Cylinder Bore . . . 1000-c.c. 2·560 in.
  600-c.c. 1·984 in.

Valve Head and Seating
  Angle . . . 45°

Gudgeon-pin :
  Diameter . . . $\left\{\begin{array}{l}0·6865 \text{ in.}\\0·6862 \text{ in.}\end{array}\right.$ (or $\frac{11}{16}$ in. −0·002 in.).

Small End Bush :
  Ream after fitting to . $\left\{\begin{array}{l}0·6868 \text{ in.}\\0·6863 \text{ in.}\end{array}\right.$ (or $\frac{11}{16}$ in. −0·001 in.).

Valve Stem :
  (Clearance in guide.)
    Inlet . . . 0·002 in.
    Exhaust . . . 0·003 in.

Crankshaft B.E. Crankpin Journal :
  Diameter . . . 1·3745 in.–1·375 in.

Connecting-rod B.E. Bearing (1937–1947 Models only) :
  Honed for fitting . . 1·3755 in.–1·376 in.

Crankshaft Plain Bearing End :
  Diameter . . . 1·2495 in.–1·250 in.

Crankshaft Plain Bearing (White Metal) :
  Honed after fitting to . 1·2515 in.–1·252 in.

Camshaft Bush in Crankcase :
  Ream after fitting to . 0·874 in.–0·875 in.

Camshaft (Bush End) :
  Diameter . . . $\left\{\begin{array}{l}0·8735\\0·873\end{array}\right.$

Crankshaft Threads :

Thread for coupling gear
extractor . . . $1\frac{3}{4}$ in. $\times$ 20 T.P.I.

Nut securing shock ab-
sorber . . . $1\frac{1}{16}$ in. $\times$ 20 T.P.I.

Nut securing front coup-
ling gear . . . $\frac{3}{4}$ in. $\times$ 20 T.P.I.

Nuts securing R.H.
crankshafts . . $\frac{3}{4}$ in. $\times$ 20 T.P.I.

Camshaft Nut . . . $\frac{3}{4}$ in. $\times$ 20 T.P.I.   Left hand.

B.E. Journal. Oil-hole . $\frac{3}{32}$ in.

Camshaft Ball Bearing :

Size . . . . $\frac{3}{4}$ in. $\times$ $1\frac{7}{8}$ in. $\times$ $\frac{9}{16}$ in.

Crankshaft Roller Bearing in Crankcase :

Two-lipped Type . 1·125 in. $\times$ $2\frac{1}{2}$ in. $\times$ $\frac{5}{8}$ in.

Crankshaft Roller Bearing in Gear Cover :

One-lipped Type . . 1·124 in. $\times$ $2\frac{1}{2}$ in. $\times$ $\frac{5}{8}$ in.

Contact-breaker Gap . 0·012 in.

Sparking-plug Point Gap . 0·015 in.–0·018 in.

Timing Chain . . . Endless $\frac{3}{8}$ in. $\times$ 67 pitches.

Magdynamo . . . Lucas Type MNIE.   180°.

Carburetter . . . Solex 26 AH.

Gear Ratios . . . Refer to Chapter VI Gearbox
Assembly.

CHAPTER III

MODEL 4/G/1000-C.C. WITH LIGHT-ALLOY ENGINE (1949–1951)

THE practice of using special light alloys for the manufacture of cylinder blocks and heads was first introduced by the Ariel concern in 1949, and the Model 4/G/1000 c.c. previously built with cast-iron cylinders and head with a separate aluminium rocker-box was discontinued and superseded by another Model 4G machine incorporating a " light-alloy " engine unit.

Construction

The early 4G engine characteristics are retained in the 1949–51 alloy unit, and as far as the lower half of the assembly is concerned many parts are identical and interchangeable.

The crankshaft assembly with connecting-rods, the latter fitted with replaceable white-metalled liners, is made up on exactly the same principle as the previous so-called " cast-iron " engine.

The camshaft, timing sprockets and chain, together with the tensioner blade arrangement, are all also very similar in design and operation to those employed in the " cast iron " unit, and therefore certain information and maintenance instructions given in this manual under the " 1937–1948 Model 4G " heading can be readily applied to the 1949–51 model.

The frame, telescopic-fork assembly, wheels, gearbox and clutch are all identical and fully interchangeable with 1937–1948 models, and all details and data with few

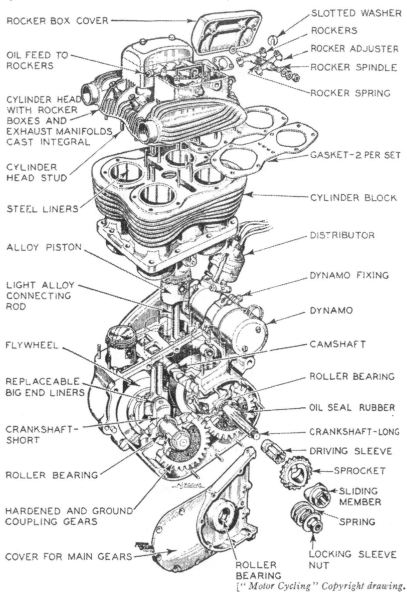

ROCKER BOX COVER

OIL FEED TO ROCKERS

CYLINDER HEAD WITH ROCKER BOXES AND EXHAUST MANIFOLDS CAST INTEGRAL

CYLINDER HEAD STUD

STEEL LINERS

ALLOY PISTON

LIGHT ALLOY CONNECTING ROD

FLYWHEEL

REPLACEABLE BIG END LINERS

CRANKSHAFT-SHORT

ROLLER BEARING

HARDENED AND GROUND COUPLING GEARS

COVER FOR MAIN GEARS

SLOTTED WASHER
ROCKERS
ROCKER ADJUSTER
ROCKER SPINDLE
ROCKER SPRING

GASKET-2 PER SET

CYLINDER BLOCK

DISTRIBUTOR

DYNAMO FIXING

DYNAMO

CAMSHAFT

ROLLER BEARING

OIL SEAL RUBBER

CRANKSHAFT-LONG

DRIVING SLEEVE

SPROCKET

SLIDING MEMBER

SPRING

LOCKING SLEEVE NUT

ROLLER BEARING

["Motor Cycling" Copyright drawing.]

FIG. 10.—EXPLODED VIEW OF THE ARIEL 4G 1000-C.C. LIGHT-ALLOY ENGINE.

exceptions can be applied to the complete range of 1000-c.c. machines.

Coil ignition with separate dynamo is employed in place of the early type Magdyno. There is no factory-sponsored coil conversion set in circulation suitable for adapting to the 1937–1948 models, neither can the standard set from the 1949–51 models be fitted on account of the fact that the crankcase of the former does not incorporate the special cradle anchorage necessary for mounting the large separate dynamo.

It must also be mentioned that the light-alloy cylinder block cannot be fitted to the crankcase of the " cast-iron " unit, which employs a different stud-base fixing.

MAINTENANCE

The Lubrication System

The lubricating system depends entirely on cleanliness, and as with all 1000-c.c. models the oil tank and crankcase sump should be drained every 1000–1500 miles and thoroughly flushed with clean petrol.

Refer to " Lubrication Recommendations " for correct grades of oil to use for 1000-c.c. models.

The oil-pressure gauge should record approximately 25–35 lb./sq. in., although a much higher pressure is permissible and is often recorded, but this indicates that the oil pump is functioning to full capacity and that the release valve is well sprung and seated. The oil pressure is controlled by a spring-loaded ball valve acting as a release when the pump produces a certain pressure limit.

The release valve is situated in the end of the front crankshaft on the timing side, and is accessible after removing the large hexagon cap in front of the chain cover.

If a low oil pressure is recorded, the release valve should be removed, dismantled and thoroughly cleaned. The small coil spring may have weakened, and a new one should be fitted for retesting. Whilst the valve is removed it is advisable to clean out as far as possible the timing end of the hollow crankshaft. Before refitting the timing-chain cover and joint washer, the complete oil pump should be removed for cleaning and checking (see Fig. 16).

Examine the steel balls and springs located below each oil-pump plunger and see that the ball seatings are clear and even. The square-head plug cups carrying the springs should be thoroughly tightened after reassembling the oil pump, and to ensure making a good joint between pump and the boss on the crankcase a new joint washer should be fitted.

It is well to note that although the rocker-box construction of the 1949–51 Model 4G varies considerably from that of the 1937–1948 type, theoretically the lubrication is identical and the diagram, Fig. 1, page 16, is applicable to all 1000-c.c. models irrespective of year of manufacture.

During the maintenance check take the opportunity to examine the timing chain, tensioner spring and blade, and the adjustable stop for blade.

The action of the stop is such that when adjusted to give approximately $\frac{1}{64}$ in. or $\frac{1}{32}$ in. clearance between it and the rear of the blade the blade cannot straighten out due to any chain snatch or irregularity which might be set up in the engine when running. Adjust the stop with engine cold and the timing chain in the tight position between sprockets.

Tappet adjustment should be checked with the engine cold and set to give 0·001 in. clearance for all inlet and exhaust valves. Note that these settings are different from those recommended for the " cast-iron " 4G engine.

Test each pair of valves for correct seating and the

tappets for clearance by rotating the engine slowly to obtain full compression on each respective cylinder when both valves should be fully closed. A safe measure to adopt is to turn the engine slightly over the full stroke in order to clear fully any cam pressure on the push-rods and rockers. The rocker adjusters can be operated with the small special spanner supplied in the tool-kit; this is also used to securely tighten the lock nuts.

The " Solex " carburetter maintenance check and adjustment details are given in a later chapter, and also those relative to the Lucas dynamo or generator (see index).

The Distributor Unit

The distributor unit of the coil-ignition system should receive a frequent maintenance check consisting of a light lubrication and adjustment of the contact-breaker rocker arm and points.

Contained in the distributor unit is a spiral drive gear and shaft engaging with the dynamo gear and all directly driven by the timing chain and sprockets in the timing case.

The contact-breaker, condenser and the automatic ignition control mechanism are all contained within the distributor unit and are readily accessible. Adjust the contact-breaker points to give the recommended gap of 0·012 in.—this can be checked with the gauge attached to the magneto spanner. Rotate the engine very slowly and watch the breaker-arm action against the cams and adjust in widest position. Wipe the actual points with a small piece of very fine emery cloth, and if they appear to have been burnt, pitted or worn uneven, remove the screw points and arm, and reface squarely with a fine magneto file or stone. Wipe the cam faces with a film of grease and drop a few spots of thin machine oil in the recess of the distributor spindle after lifting off the keyed rotor arm. Also put a few drops of oil in the external lubricator, if fitted, approximately every 3000 miles.

Check to ensure that the H.T. carbon brush inside the distributor cover is clean and freely sprung to make good contact with the metal segment on the rotor arm. The rotor is a push fit and keyed to the centre driving spindle and can be lifted off and replaced easily by finger pressure.

All cable connections, terminals and securing nuts, etc., incorporated in the coil-ignition system should receive a periodical maintenance check.

DECARBONISATION

Removing Cylinder-Head with Integral Rocker-Boxes

With a new machine after a " running-in " mileage of approximately 2000 it is advisable to lift the cylinder-head for the initial decarbonisation and to enable all the valves and seatings to be carefully examined and lightly reground. Afterwards a mileage of 8000–10,000 can be covered before a further decarbonisation is necessary, providing of course the engine performance has not been affected in any way.

For ease of operation the petrol tank should be raised or completely removed, as this leaves the procedure of dismantling the carburetter, rocker-box covers and oil pipe, etc., more easy and accessible. Next remove the eight head-securing nuts from the cylinder-block studs which pass upwards and through the holes in the head casting.

Four nuts are located inside the rocker-boxes and four outside. Next take notice that there are twelve more securing nuts located between the second and third cylinder-block fins, these being screwed to the studs fixed into the cylinder-head. Unscrew these nuts almost to the ends of the studs and lift the alloy cylinder-head far enough to allow a few thin strips of metal or spanners to be inserted to support the head whilst the twelve nuts are finally removed from between the fins (see Fig. 11).

If any difficulty is experienced in loosening the cylinder-

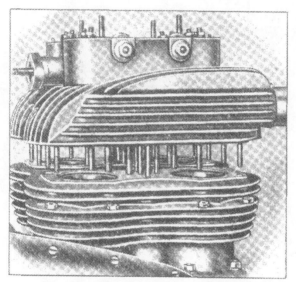

FIG. 11.——CYLINDER-HEAD REMOVAL.
Twelve nuts securing cylinder-head are situated between second and third cylinder-block fins.

head from the block, try rotating the engine with the kick-starter, leaving the sparking plugs in position to give full compression. The H.T. cables should be disconnected. This operation should have the effect of breaking the joint, which may be sealed tightly by the head gasket. Do not on any account attempt to prise up the head with metal tools, as the light-alloy faces can be easily damaged. Pull out the push-rods and suitably mark each one to ensure that they can be replaced in the same order.

Unless a top overhaul is considered necessary, the

cylinder block need not be removed for decarbonisation, but all carbon can be cleaned from the piston tops after rotating the engine slowly in order to bring each piston to T.D.C. position as required.

It is not necessary to remove the rockers unless wear is suspected, and then the operation is very simple and only necessitates removing the rocker-spindle end nuts

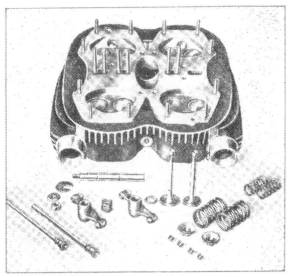

FIG. 12.—CYLINDER-HEAD WITH VALVE AND ROCKER FITTINGS.

on the outside of the box casting and then gently punching each spindle a short distance along the housings.

The slotted washers locating the spindles inside the rocker-box can now be removed and the spindles withdrawn.

Before dismantling the rocker assembly it is advisable to take note of the order of position of the respective springs and rocker thrust washers (see Fig. 12).

Do not on any account immerse the cylinder-head in any form of caustic solution to remove carbon, because although this is common practice with cast-iron heads and blocks, caustic soda solutions will very quickly entirely ruin any aluminium or allied alloy. Decarbonise the head with the aid of wire brushes and scrapers only, taking care not to damage valve seatings and guides.

Valve seatings are formed in the light-alloy material by pressing in separate inserts manufactured from a high-expansion steel. No attempt should be made to replace the inserts unless equipped with suitable tools and knowledge of such procedure. Note also that the valve guides are not of the usual cast-iron type, being made up from bored bronze bar and securely held in position by the valve-spring pressure. In order to prevent damage to the alloy material through tightening sparking plugs, bronze bush inserts are pressed into the head to receive any standard 14-mm. plug.

Valves have heat-treated stem ends, and therefore the hardened end caps as used on the " cast-iron " model 4G are not necessary.

Reassembling

After the head has been thoroughly cleaned and all valves correctly ground in to their respective seatings, a new gasket or joint washer should be prepared and placed in position on the top face of the cylinder block, which should also have been thoroughly cleaned. Do not use jointing compound. Assuming now that the rockers and valves are all correctly assembled again, the head complete is ready for refitting. Replace the twelve securing nuts between the second and third fins of the block and position them immediately below the corresponding stud holes in the block face ready to receive the screwed ends of the studs when the cylinder-head is lowered into position.

Insert the push-rods into the head and locate with each respective rocker arm before fitting the head, which when lowered into position will allow the extreme ends of the twelve studs to engage the securing nuts.

Before attempting to screw on the nuts further, lift the head approximately ⅛ in. and insert two of the metal strips or thin spanners to support it whilst screwing the nuts on a further few threads.

Remove the strips and finally tighten up all twelve nuts between the fins, not forgetting the eight which bear against the top of the cylinder-head.

When tightening the head-securing nuts it is essential to screw down the nuts to almost full travel and then to finally tighten each in a cross-over action from corner to corner, etc., commencing with the eight centre ones. It is absolutely necessary to ensure that a perfect head joint is made, and therefore it is advisable to always re-tighten the securing nuts after warming up the engine and again after approximately 100 miles running.

The valve clearances should be set as described under " Maintenance " and checked again after retightening the head-securing nuts.

DISMANTLING ENGINE FOR COMPLETE OVERHAUL

Removal of Engine from Frame

The complete engine unit can be removed from the frame in exactly the same manner as the 1937–1948 1000-c.c. models, and all instructions for this operation together with those for dismantling the clutch assembly, etc., will be found on pages 25 and 115.

Removing Engine-Shaft Shock Absorber

After the clutch and outer primary-chain cover have been removed the shock-absorber assembly will be exposed, and it will be noted that the design of this has been changed from that of all previous 4G models. A two-cam sliding member and corresponding engine sprocket is fitted in place of the original three-cam type, thus giving a far more sensitive and responsive action to the transmission. A splined driving sleeve and sleeve-type nut is fitted in place of the early pattern tab washer and lock-nut device. Note the order of assembly, see exploded view of engine unit (Fig. 10) and also see when dismantling the exact location of the self-aligning—rubber and spring—oil seal. Refer to page 25 for instructions relating to previous models. For the benefit of owners of all 1937–1948 1000-c.c. machines it is quite possible and permissible to fit the above-mentioned modified engine-shaft shock-absorber assembly complete, as well as the oil seal, to all existing units without any alteration to the splined shaft or coupling gear.

Crankshaft Assembly Coupling Gears

The main coupling gears are identical to those fitted to all previous 1000-c.c. models, and therefore reference can be made to pages 27–29 for a description of the procedure to adopt for removing and reassembling them (see Fig. 13).

Direct lubrication for the coupling gears is provided by a small feed pipe directing a constant flow of oil on to them at the teeth-engaging position.

Removing Timing Gear

The timing gear lay-out is similar to that of the 1937–1948 models, except the 6-volt Lucas dynamo is driven by a different type of sprocket from that previously fitted for driving the Magdyno unit.

An adjustable tensioner blade stop is employed to give a more constant chain tension, and this arrangement has already been described under " Maintenance ".

A fibre rubbing strip is not fitted inside the timing chest as on previous models, and is not necessary with the adjustable type tensioner.

The crankshaft and dynamo sprockets can be removed with the aid of the small special extractor supplied by

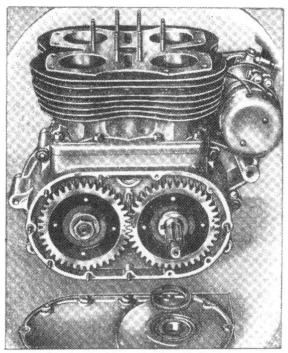

FIG. 13.——CRANKSHAFT COUPLING GEARS.
Showing timing marks and self-adjusting oil seal.

the makers in the tool-kit. The camshaft nut and oil-pump drive is left-hand thread, the sprocket being keyed to the same shaft and a tight push fit. No extractor is necessary for removing the camshaft sprocket, and only a very light leverage need be applied.

The oil pump and drive is identical to that of the 1937–1948 models and has also been described (see " Maintenance "). Note that there should be a maximum

clearance of 0·005 in. only between the rear face of the
Dural sliding block of the oil pump and the front face
of the camshaft nut. Any excess clearance at this point
will cause a mechanical tapping noise to be set up whilst
running; provision is made for thin packing shims to be
fitted between the camshaft sprocket and the securing
nut until clearance is correct. To ensure being able at
any time to make a leakproof joint always keep a new
oil-pump washer in reserve.

The dynamo and distributor have already been described, and can be withdrawn as a complete unit after
unscrewing the securing stud. See also " Electrical
Equipment ".

Removing the Cylinder Block

After removing the cylinder-head (see Fig. 11) as
described under " Decarbonisation ", it is a very straightforward operation to take off the cylinder block. There
are twelve $\frac{5}{16}$-in. securing base nuts all quite accessible
for removing now that the dynamo has been taken off.
Rotate the engine until all pistons are more or less at the
same level, and raise the block carefully until the four
pistons are free. The cylinder block is cast in aluminium–
silicon light alloy and fitted with press-fit liners manufactured from a special nickel iron with a tested expansion
rate equal to the block.

Piston clearances can be closer than those specified for
the cast-iron assembly without any risk of seizure (see
pages 56–58 for full " Data "). Two compression and one
slotted-type rings are fitted to each piston. If in course
of time the cylinder liners show signs of wear and piston
clearances increase, the bores can be reground to a
0·020 in. maximum oversize and pistons matched to
suit. When, after lengthy service, a second rebore

becomes necessary, preference should be given to the fitting of new liners and standard pistons.

Pistons, Gudgeon-pins and Small-end Bushes

Except for piston clearance on the light-alloy unit (see " Data ") all details under these headings contained in Chapter II are also relative to all the 1000-c.c. models.

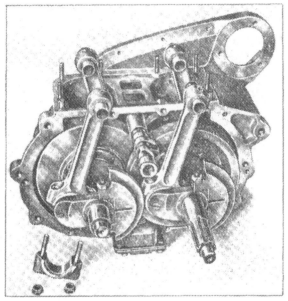

FIG. 14.—CONNECTING-RODS AND CRANKSHAFT
ASSEMBLY.

Checking Main Bearings

Although the 1949–51 crankcases differ slightly from the 1937–1948 type, the fundamental principles of design and lay-out are identical, and therefore the description and instructions for dismantling can be considered relative for the light-alloy unit (see pages 29–30).

Connecting-rods

All rods are fitted with loose-shell-type liners for big-end bearings (see Fig. 14). Each bearing should be tested for diametrical clearance due to wear, and if 0·003 in.–0·004 in. is exceeded, new liners should be fitted. If after lengthy service, fitting new liners does not reduce clearance to the safe maximum figure, then the crank journals should be checked for ovality and total wear and reground until a uniform diameter is found. Special under-size-in-the-bore liners are obtainable from the makers for fitting to reground crank journals. When refitting the connecting-rods and liners note that the key on each half-shell engages correctly with the slot in each respective rod and end cap and that the cap is replaced in the correct position as indicated by the stamped markings.

Camshaft Bush and Bearing

These should be checked for wear, and if found necessary to remove the bush for renewal, proceed as per instructions given on page 33.

Reassembling the Crankshafts

As previously mentioned the assembly and procedure for dismantling is identical to that for the 1937–1948 models, and reference can therefore be made to pages 29–31 for the few simple instructions covering the operation.

Refitting the Cylinder Block

It is advisable to replace the block before refitting the timing gear and dynamo so that full access can be given to the rear cylinder-base-securing nuts. Pistons and fittings having been dealt with previously and now refitted to the connecting-rods, the block can be prepared for lifting into position as described on pages 24–25.

Tappets and Guides

Do not disturb these unless lengthy service and wear make it necessary to replace. Check, however, the four

tappet guide blocks to ensure that these are a snug fit in
the block and see that the guide-securing plates are
perfectly flat and not distorted in any way. These
plates should be refaced by rubbing down on a surface
plate. Also check the two tab lock washers, and when
assembling securely tighten the securing nuts (see
Fig. 15).

Timing Gear—Reassembling

First securely refix the dynamo and distributor unit in
the cradle housing.

Examine the timing chain for wear and stretch and
replace if necessary (Fig. 16).

Valve Timing.—This is also identical to that of the
1937–1948 models, and the method for timing as described on page 33 can be applied. One or two attempts
may be necessary in order to obtain a correct fine limit
timing, and to get the best results it is advisable to gently
withdraw the dynamo and camshaft sprockets from their
respective shafts and mesh with the chain on a trial-and-
error method. When correct meshing is obtained, fit
all sprockets securely and adjust the tensioner blade stop
as previously described.

Ignition Timing

Contained in the distributor unit is the automatic
control mechanism governing the retard and advance
position, and when stationary the control is always fully
retarded, being held thus by internal springs.

If the distributor unit has been withdrawn from the
dynamo during the overhaul it can be re-engaged quite
easily by gently turning the driving spindle until the
attached skew gear slides into mesh with a corresponding
gear on the dynamo armature. Before meshing, however, see that the contact-breaker points are only just

FIG. 15.—TAPPET ARRANGEMENT IN CYLINDER
BLOCK.

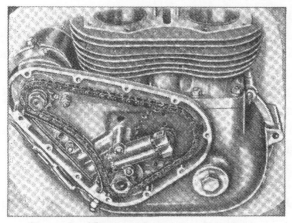

FIG. 16.—TIMING GEAR AND OIL PUMP.
Valve timing method is described on page 33.

separating when No. 1 piston—front right-hand side—is
at T.D.C. and with the distributor-head flat portion in
line with the side of the oil tank.

The distributor can be finally adjusted to a fine setting
by unscrewing the clip bolt and rotating the unit either
in a clockwise direction to retard or anti-clockwise to
further the advance position.

After correctly timing No. 1 cylinder—front right-hand
—all the H.T. leads should be checked for condition
and renewed if showing signs of cracking, etc.   Note
carefully the order of cable distribution and mark each
one for future identification.   If a new set of H.T. leads
is to be fitted trace each point of connection in relation
to the rotor contact and connect to the sparking plugs in
the order of firing which is Nos. 1, 2, 3, 4 clockwise
around the cylinder-head.

Coil ignition is often liable to give trouble when the
various components are exposed to the elements, as they
are when fitted to a motor cycle, and therefore it is wise
to take the precaution to cover the distributor head and
cables with some suitable waterproofing, such as a rubber
sheath or oiled-silk sheeting.

Also note that it is essential to keep the main coil lead
well away from the frame of the cycle in order to prevent
any rubbing and subsequent leakage of H.T. current.

See also page 36 for similar hints regarding waterproofing.

DATA FOR 1949-51 1000-c.c. MODEL 4G
(With Light-Alloy Cylinder Block and Head)

Engine :
  Bore, 65 mm.
  Stroke, 75 mm.
  Capacity Actual, 997 c.c.
  B.H.P. at 5400 r.p.m., 34·5.
  Compression Ratio, 6·0 to 1.

Valve Timing :

    Inlet Valve opens (before T.D.C.), $\frac{3}{16}$ in. or 25°.
    Inlet Valve closes (after B.D.C.), $\frac{1}{2}$ in. or 55°.
    Exhaust Valve opens (before B.D.C.), $\frac{19}{32}$ in. or 60°.
    Exhaust Valve closes (after T.D.C.), $\frac{1}{8}$ in. or 20°.

Ignition Timing : Piston T.D.C. Automatic control fully retarded, *i.e.*, normal with engine idle, Contact Points just breaking.

Oil Pressure : (Non-Adjustable.) Max. 35 lb./sq. in., min. 25 lb./sq. in.

Valve Clearance :

    With Engine Cold.   Inlet Valve, 0·001 in.
                           Exhaust Valve, 0·001 in.

Piston-Ring Gap :

    Compression Rings, 0·012 in.–0·017 in.
    Oil-Control Ring, 0·015 in.–0·020 in.

Piston Clearance in Cyl. Bore :

    Ring Land, 0·020 in.–0·023 in.
    Below Rings, 0·003 in.–0·005 in.
    Extreme Skirt, 0·001 in.–0·003 in.

Cylinder Bore : 2·559 in.

Valve Head and Seating Angle : 45°.

Gudgeon Pin : Diameter, 0·6865 in.–0·6862 in. (or $\frac{11}{16}$ in. minus 0·002 in.).

Small-End Bush : Ream after fitting to 0·6868 in.–0·6863 in. (or $\frac{11}{16}$ in. minus 0·001 in.).

Valve Stem :

    Inlet.   Diameter, 0·311 in.–0·312 in.
    Exhaust.   Diameter, 0·309 in.–0·310 in.

Valve Guide : Inlet and Exhaust. Internal Bore, 0·313 in.–0·314 in.

Rocker Arm : Internal Bore, 0·4995 in.–0·5005 in.

Rocker Spindle : Diameter, 0·498 in.–0·499 in.

Crankshaft Big-End Journal : Diameter, 1·3745 in.–1·375 in.

Crankshaft, Plain Bearing End : Diameter, 1·2495 in.–1·250 in.

Crankshaft Plain Bearing (White Metal) : Honed after fitting to, 1·2515 in.–1·252 in.

Camshaft Bush in Crankcase : Ream after fitting to, 0·874 in.–
0·875 in.

Camshaft (Bush End) : Diameter, 0·8735 in.–0·873 in.

Camshaft Nut : ¾ in. × 20 T.P.I.   (Left Hand.)

Crankshaft Threads :
Thread on Coupling Gears for Extractor, 1¾ in. × 20 T.P.I.
Sleeve Nut securing shock absorber, ⅞ in. × 20 T.P.I.
Nut securing front coupling gear, ¾ in. × 20 T.P.I.
Nuts securing crankshafts right-hand or timing side, ¾ in.
× 20 T.P.I.

Camshaft Ball Bearing : Size ¾ in. × 1⅞ in. × ⁹⁄₁₆ in.

Crankshaft Roller Bearing in Crankcase : Lipped Type, 1·125 in.
× 2½ in. × ⅜ in.   (2 off.)

Crankshaft Roller Bearing in Gear Cover : Lipped Type,
1·124 in. × 2½ in. × ⅜ in.   (1 off.)

Timing Chain : (Endless) ⅜ in. × 67 Pitches.

Contact-Breaker Gap (Coil Ignition) : 0·012 in.

Sparking-Plug Point Gap (Coil Ignition) : 0·025 in.

Carburetter : Solex—BiStarter—Type 26AH.

CHAPTER IV

500-C.C. TWIN-CYLINDER MODELS "KG" AND "KH" (1948–51)

THE model "KG" Standard De Luxe and the model "KH" "Red Hunter" 500-c.c. vertical twin-cylinder models were first introduced for the 1948 season. The two models are basically identical, except for certain details associated with equipment and finish.

Construction

The "KH" incorporates a polished cylinder-head and ports, and there is a slight difference in the Amal carburetter mixing chamber and main jet from those of the "KG".

High-compression pistons are available as extras from the manufacturers for fitting to the model "KH", and are most suitable for use with any good high-octane fuel. With 70–72 octane Pool fuel the standard piston is advised for both power units (see "Data" for compression ratios, etc., pages 81–82).

The frame and telescopic-fork assemblies are the same for both models. The fork is the Ariel standard as fitted to all single- and four-cylinder machines, but the frame is a slightly lightened type and not interchangeable with others in the Ariel range (see Chapters VIII and X).

The well-known Ariel rear spring-frame attachment can be fitted to models "KG" and "KH" frames during the course of manufacture only of new machines.

The gearbox is Burman standard and fully interchangeable throughout the Ariel range (see Chapter VI).

Ignition is by B.T.H. or Lucas twin-type magneto,

both fitted with automatic advance and retard mechanism of the governor and spring-control pattern.

A separate Lucas 6-volt dynamo is used for lighting, etc.

Lubrication

Engine lubrication is by a dual-geared-type oil pump in the crankcase sump, which is completely enclosed in a fine-mesh filter positioned by a coiled spring and readily accessible by way of a detachable base plate beneath the crankcase. Oil reaches the delivery side of the pump by gravity feed from a separate oil tank, and is then forced along internal oilways to a white-metal-lined bush in the timing side of the crankcase. From this main crankshaft bush or bearing, the oil, now under pump pressure, enters the hollow crankshaft and feeds the big-end bearings by way of suitably drilled holes in the two crank ournals.

Oil pressure is kept constant by a non-adjustable relief valve fitted into the end of the crankshaft on the timing side and designed to show a pressure on the gauge of approximately 25 lb./sq. in. with normal running.

An external oil pipe-line is taken to the cylinder-head and rocker-box assembly and fed to the rocker spindles, etc., through a four-way copper-pipe assembly. From the cylinder-head the oil drops down inside the push-rod channels—cast in with the cylinder block—and into the main crankcase, thus thoroughly lubricating all tappets and camshafts. The amount of oil released into the crankcase is sufficient for the crankshaft and flywheel to throw upwards for splash lubrication of both pistons.

Two large-diameter holes in the timing-side crankcase also allow oil to be blown into the timing-gear case for lubricating the gear and chain. A drain hole is provided at a determined level also in the timing-side half-case through which any excess oil is passed back into the main case sump, filter and return side of the pump to be subsequently sent back into the separate oil-storage tank.

Excess crankcase pressure is released in the form of oil mist via a light, spring-loaded ball-valve breather situated immediately above the oil-pump driving spindle and to which is attached a union and copper pipe leading to the rear driving chain for slight extra lubrication purposes.

A skew gear on the top end of the long oil-pump driving spindle engages with a worm gear machined on the rear or inlet camshaft and constitutes a positive drive for the geared oil pump.

Valve Gear

Two separate camshafts are employed, each serving a dual purpose by operating the respective inlet and exhaust tappets and also carrying the timing-chain sprockets with magneto- and dynamo-driven gears. The front or exhaust camshaft carries a chain sprocket to which is attached the dynamo fabric gear suitably mounted with a " slipping-clutch " friction-drive arrangement. The rear or inlet camshaft carries a chain sprocket to which is riveted another fabric gear for meshing with the steel driving gear of the magneto. Attached to this gear is the automatic advance and retard mechanism.

Overhead rockers are push-rod operated and transmit pressure direct to the usual orthodox valve lay-out in the cylinder-head.

MAINTENANCE

Maintenance adjustments for the twin engine consist of the type associated with any internal-combustion air-cooled motor-cycle unit, and apply chiefly to valve or rocker clearances, magneto, carburetter and the lubrica-

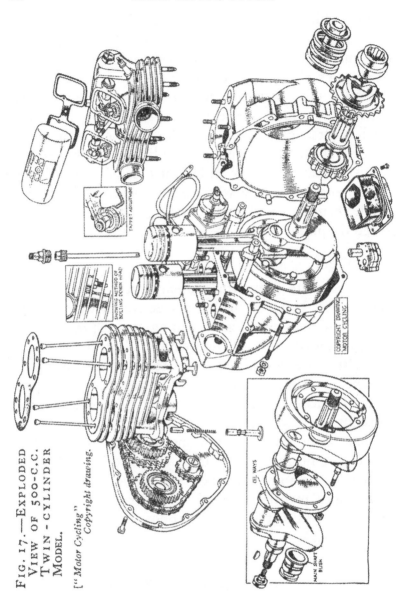

FIG. 17.—EXPLODED VIEW OF 500-C.C. TWIN-CYLINDER MODEL.

["Motor Cycling" Copyright drawing.

tion system.   Reference should be made to the data chart, pages 81–82, for correct tappet and other settings, and attention given to the lubrication system according to the mileage and conditions under which the machine is used.

Generally speaking, it is advisable to check the tappets every 500–600 miles, and to drain and cleanse the oil tank, crankcase sump and filter every 1000 miles.

Lubrication System

The oil pump should not be removed unnecessarily during maintenance procedure, and providing the system is kept clean the pump should not fail to operate, being, as afore-mentioned, positively driven direct from the geared camshaft.   A higher oil-gauge reading than 25 lb. may be recorded when the engine is cold, but this merely indicates that all is well with the pump, etc., and full delivery is taking place.   If the oil-tank filler cap is removed whilst the engine is running, the action of the return side of the pump can be checked by observing the flow of oil being pumped back into the tank.

Should the oil gauge fail to register, carefully check over the following points :

Make certain that the supply tank and the filter beneath the filler cap are clean and the oil level in the tank is correct.   Check for leakage all oil-pipe connections to gauge and cylinder-head.

Check the delivery and return pipe-lines from the oil tank to crankcase, and ensure that no air leakage is present on the supply side.

Test the oil gauge pipe for clearance internally by inserting a length of fine wire.

If all is well with pipe-lines, etc., and engine running pressure is low or nil but oil is actually returning to the tank, then it might be assumed that there is an internal pressure leakage by way of the relief valve in the end of the crankshaft.   Check the valve by first removing the timing-gear cover, and then unscrew the valve body complete from the end of the shaft (see Fig. 17).   Take out the split cotter pin, spring and steel ball from the valve body and cleanse in clean petrol and ensure that the steel ball makes good contact in the seating. If the original appears distorted or weakened fit a new spring and reassemble, but, before refitting the complete valve to the crankshaft, clean out from the hollow oil-way any residue of foreign matter which may have accumulated.

If after a retest no pressure is recorded, the oil pump can be removed for examination by taking off the bottom crankcase sump plate, gauze filter and spring, and then removing the pump's four securing screws and gently pulling the complete oil pump out of the crankcase housing.

Dismantle the pump, if it appears to be tight or locked, by unscrewing the pins securing the body sections and pulling them apart so as to expose the internal gear pinions. Check the condition of the pinions and spindles and wash thoroughly in petrol. Re-assemble with new joint washers and ensure that the pump can be rotated freely by hand.

When fitting the pump back into the crankcase make sure to engage correctly the tongue and slot of the long driving shaft and short pump spindle before finally tightening the four securing screws. Prime the sump well with clean oil before fitting the bottom plate and testing.

Tappet Adjustment

The four tappets (1948/9 models) are spring loaded to ensure silent operation (see Fig. 17) and adjustment of the recommended 0·002 in. clearance for the inlet and exhaust is carried out with the engine cold and valves closed.

The 1950/51 models are fitted with integral tappets which are not spring loaded.

To test for clearance each rocker arm should be lifted,

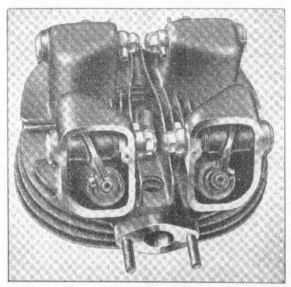

FIG. 18.—TAPPET ARRANGEMENT 1951 TWIN-CYLINDER 500-C.C. "KG" AND "KH" MODELS.

FIG. 18a.—METHOD OF REMOVING VALVES.

that is away from the valve-stem end, by putting pressure on the spring tappet. With a rocker arm held thus a " feeler " gauge should be inserted and clearance noted.

The 1948/50 and early series of 1951 models are fitted with rocker arms incorporating clamp pins to secure the rocker-adjusting screws, and the makers provided a small socket key in the kit for loosening the clamp and also for adjusting the rocker screw. Late 1951 models are fitted with rocker adjusters and ordinary lock nuts, both operated by a small special flat spanner from the kit.

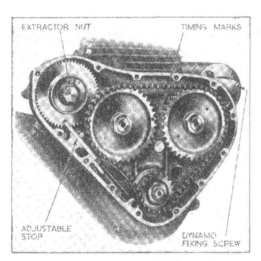

FIG. 19.—TIMING GEAR SHOWING ADJUST-ABLE STOP PLATE.

After adjusting and finally checking the clearances, either the clamp screws or the lock nuts should be very carefully tightened. The illustration, Fig. 18 shows the positions of the clamp-screw-type adjusters.

Timing-Chain Tensioner

The timing gear and chain cover should be removed occasionally and the spring chain tensioner examined for clearance. There will be seen in position an adjustable stop plate (Fig. 19) with which the spring blade contacts with a buffer action. Wear or stretch of the timing chain will make adjustment of the stop plate necessary, and with the engine stationary and the chain in the tightest position—ascertained by rocking the timing gear slightly—the stop plate should be set to allow 0·010 in. clearance only between the plate end and the contacting end of the blade. To ensure quiet action of the timing gear do not allow excess clearance ever to set up, otherwise a loud metallic knock very similar to that caused by a badly adjusted tappet will occur, or it can even be mistaken for " piston slap ".

DECARBONISATION

After " running in " a new or re-conditioned engine, during which period an excess of carbon and burnt-oil deposits are built up within the cylinder-head combustion chambers, the head should be removed for cleaning and examination at approximately 2000–3000 miles.

With normal running after this first decarbonisation a further mileage of 8000 can be covered before dismantling the cylinder-head again.

The twin-cylinder engine is very prone to " pinking " if allowed to carbonise, and the above mileage should not be exceeded during the periods.

Removing the Cylinder-Head

Take off or raise and prop up the petrol tank for ease of operation after disconnecting the centre oil-gauge pipe.

Next remove the petrol pipe, or pipes on 1950/51 models, the oil pipe from crankcase to centre union on cylinder-head, then the carburetter, exhaust pipes and rocker-box covers.

Do not disturb the four-way oil-pipe assembly to the rocker spindles (see Fig. 18a). Note where the eight cylinder-head fixing nuts are located in between the second and third cylinder-block fins, and with a thin open-end set spanner release the nuts by five or six turns.

Have in readiness two thin spanners for packing between the head and the top face of the cylinder block when the head has been lifted sufficiently to allow the eight fixing studs to almost clear the second fin of the block. The nuts can then be finally released and allowed to settle between the fins (see Fig. 20). Whilst the cylinder-head is being lifted, hold the four push-rods in position in their respective rockers until they are clear of the block, when the complete head can be withdrawn sideways.

FIG. 20.—REMOVING THE CYLINDER-HEAD.

Note the position of nuts between the fins.

Withdraw the push-rods and mark them for identification purposes when reassembling.

An O.H.V. valve-spring compressor, which can be purchased from any good-class accessory dealer, is essential for removing the four valves which are secured with the usual common type split cones (see Fig. 18a).

Mark all valves and fittings and replace them in the same order. Decarbonisation of the cylinder-head is carried out in the usual way by scraping or wire brushing, and grinding the valves into their respective seatings with a good-quality compound.

The four overhead rockers need not be removed for decarbonisation purposes, and they can be held away from the valve-stem ends in order to allow clearance for the forked or cup end of the compressor tool.

Note that the separate hardened valve-stem end caps are not used on the twin-cylinder models; all stems being scientifically treated to withstand hard wear and tear.

Do not attempt to replace the valves into the head until it is certain that all seatings are in perfect order and all trace of carbon has been removed and the combustion chambers and ports thoroughly washed.

Have in readiness a replacement cylinder-head joint washer or gasket, because after once being disturbed it is sometimes difficult to obtain a good oil- and gas-tight joint by using an already compressed or distorted gasket.

Both pistons can be brought to T.D.C. by a turn of the engine, and all carbon should be removed from the crowns by scraping. It is not necessary to remove the cylinder block for a common decarbonisation, but if it is thought desirable to examine the pistons and rings, reference should be made to later notes (see page 72 under " Dismantling Complete Engine ").

Refitting the Cylinder-Head

After preparing the complete head for reassembly, and having ascertained that the head and block faces are perfectly clean, the new gasket should be placed in position, but without the use of jointing compound.

Note the exact position of the eight head nuts placed between the fins of the block, and observe that each head stud has a radius at the end to assist engagement with the corresponding nuts. Place the push-rods in position in the head, making quite sure that they can be located easily with the rocker arms, and lift the head into position and at the same time enter the lower ends of the push-rods into their respective channels in the block.

Replace the thin spanners or other suitable packing pieces on the cylinder-block face and lower the head to rest on them whilst engagement of the fixing studs and nuts is carried out. After turning the nuts two or three times on to the studs, remove the packings and tighten up equally. After each decarbonisation, it is advisable before refitting the carburetter to dismantle it completely and wash out the jets and passages and examine and replace, if necessary, the two flange washers which are to be positioned one each side of the induction distance piece. Check the tappets and set clearances to 0·002 in. as previously described. Run the engine for a short period to warm it up, then again check and tighten the head-fixing nuts, and after the initial run on the road make a further check and again tighten if possible. Repeat the tightening process several times during the next 1000 miles until the new head gasket has been well " bedded down ". Tappet adjustment should also be checked several times.

Carburetter, Magneto and Dynamo Data and Maintenance

Reference should be made to the index for information on these subjects.

DISMANTLING COMPLETE ENGINE

No hard-and-fast ruling can be given regarding the exact mileage to be covered before a complete engine overhaul is necessary. So much depends upon the type of service to which the machine has been subjected, but generally speaking, if run under normal conditions a well-maintained engine unit should not require a full overhaul at less than 20,000 miles.

To remove the engine unit from the frame it is not essential to take off the petrol tank unless it is desired to do so for ease of operation.   After removing the exhaust pipes, carburetter, battery, oil-gauge pipe, oil tank and pipes, etc., the complete clutch, primary chaincase and engine shock absorber should be entirely dismantled. Refer to notes under " Gearbox and Clutch Assembly " for instructions relative to taking apart the clutch.

When the outer half of the chaincase is removed the engine-shaft shock absorber is exposed, and it will be noticed that this assembly is held in position by a locking sleeve nut.

The order of assembling should be observed at the time of dismantling, and is as follows :

   (1) splined driving sleeve with crankcase oil seal next to roller bearing;

   (2) engine driving sprocket;

   (3) sliding member;

   (4) spring;

   (5) spring-retaining plate;

   (6) hardened washer;

   (7) sleeve locking nut.

After the chaincase, etc., has been taken away, remove all the engine-plate tie bolts, first taking the precaution to support the engine by placing a suitable packing block or box under the crankcase. The engine, now having been lifted clear, should be held securely in a bench vice or otherwise supported ready for removing the cylinder-head and cylinder block. Dismantling the head has already been dealt with under " Decarbonisation ".

Removing the Cylinder Block

To remove the twin cylinder block, rotate the engine by turning the driving mainshaft in order to bring both pistons at B.D.C., and then take off all cylinder-base securing nuts. As the cylinder block is reversible, take care to mark " Front " or " Rear " before removing.

When lifting the block from the crankcase, be careful to see that the spring-loaded tappets, if fitted, do not foul the crankcase housings in which they operate, and also see that the pistons come away from their respective bores quite freely. If tappet wear is suspected, pull each one out of the cylinder block and mark for reference when refitting. Each tappet stem, on 1948/49 models only, consists of two separate parts with a coil spring between, and is positioned in the channel of the block by a small circlip. Examine each circular tappet " foot " for wear and check stems and guides (see " Technical Data ").

Servicing Cylinder Bores and Pistons

Carefully examine both cylinder bores for wear or score markings. If piston " slap " has been suspected and the bores can be gauged to show excessive wear, especially at the top of the stroke position and exceeding 0·008 in., then a rebore is advisable. In any case, the practice of fitting a new piston to a worn bore is not recommended, and if the pistons show any signs of wear at a 20,000-mile overhaul, then the bores should be reground to 0·020 in. oversize and suitable pistons, complete with rings and pins, fitted.

Refer to " Technical Data " for piston clearances and ring gaps. The makers' recommendation for a maximum oversize is 0·040 in., but they undertake a standard of 0·020 in. only and supply pistons to suit.

Gudgeon-pin circlips can be removed with a sharp-pointed scriber-type tool, and when once taken out should always be discarded and new, correctly-tensioned ones fitted.

Gudgeon-pin and small-end-bush clearances should not exceed 0·003 in., and the data chart gives correct sizes for checking purposes. Small-end bushes are a tight fit

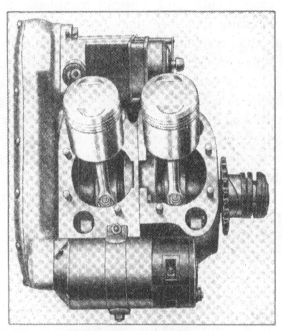

FIG. 21.—ARRANGEMENT OF PISTONS, MAGNETO, DYNAMO AND SHOCK-ABSORBER ASSEMBLY.

in the connecting-rods, but can be withdrawn by using a light press or an extractor made up from a draw bolt, nut and an old bush of less diameter. New bushes can be pressed or drawn in by the same method reversed and can then be reamed to size—always after fitting.

The pistons are removed by supporting each one in turn on one side and then driving out the gudgeon-pin from the opposite side with a suitable short-length drift or punch, or an old gudgeon-pin ground to a smaller diameter.

Removing Timing Gears and Chain

The timing gears and chain must be removed before attempting to dismantle the crankcases, but before doing so the position of the timing marks—centre-punch dots—should be carefully recorded and so assist in obtaining a correct setting when reassembling. After taking away the tensioner blade and spring complete, the three sprocket-securing nuts are next removed from the two camshafts and crankshaft end. A special screwed or threaded type sprocket extractor and draw bolt is supplied by the makers for withdrawing the sprockets; but although it is advisable to use three of these to draw the sprockets off gradually and all together complete with endless chain in position, the operation can be carried out with one tool or even with the aid of the ordinary pattern gear puller as used in the car industry.

Check the timing chain, after cleaning, for stretch and wear by pulling on short sections of it and carefully noting the amount of slack between the links. After lengthy mileage renew the chain, and thus ensure a correct valve and ignition timing (see Fig. 19).

When sprockets are removed take note if any end-play packing shims are present in the recess of each timing gear, as these will perhaps be necessary again when reassembling. Note also the position of the hardened end-thrust washer on the crankshaft end, and also of the position behind this washer of any packing shims which may have been used to determine correct end play.

The crankshaft and camshaft location for end play is dealt with under " Reassembly ".

Removing the Magneto and Dynamo

Magneto removal comes next, and is easily carried out by unscrewing the special extractor nut on the armature spindle; this will withdraw the complete automatic advance and retard control unit.   Examine this unit and ensure that the springs do not show signs of weakening or fracture.   The makers supply control units complete, and it is not advisable to attempt any repair to them, except perhaps to renew a spring.   The magneto is located against the rear face of the crankcase timing chest by a flange and three fixing nuts which are unscrewed for final removal of the unit.

These notes apply to either B.T.H. or Lucas magnetos.

Dynamo removal is carried out by releasing the securing strap and the nut close to the chain cover and sliding the unit out complete with the small steel driving gear attached.

Engine Overhaul

Remove next the crankcase sump plate, filter and oil pump as previously dealt with under " Maintenance ".

Take off the crankcase pressure-release valve and pipe to rear chain.   The crankcase halves are ready for parting after releasing all fixing studs and nuts and the two very important internal fixing bolts just below the top cylinder face of the crankcase.

The crankcase can be parted by gently tapping with a workshop hide hammer or mallet, and the shaft and camshafts can then be taken out.

The connecting-rods are removed by taking off the pinnacle-type nuts from the securing bolts and pulling the main part of the rod(s) away.   Note very carefully how the big-end shell liners are located, and mark the rods and end caps to ensure that they are replaced in the same order.   Check the condition of the shell liners and crank journals, and if either journal registers ovality at all, it should be reground to a permissible 0·010 in. undersize and small-diameter liners fitted.

Big-end-bearing shell liners are replaceable in pairs only, and when new should register clearance of 0·0005 in.–

0·001 in. when fitted to the rods and tried on the journals. Each complete rod assembly should show end clearance or float of approximately 0·020 in.

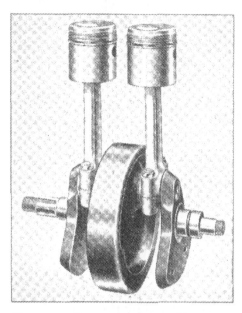

FIG. 22.—CRANKSHAFT AND CONNECT-
ING-ROD ASSEMBLY.

Crankshaft internal oilways should be thoroughly cleared after removing the screwed plugs and pressure-relief valve.

Wash out with clean paraffin or petrol and pass a stiff piece of wire through the holes to prove that all is well.

All 1948/49 models incorporated crank-shafts with a small oil-feed hole in each big-end journal, but so as to improve internal and piston lubrication on the 1950/51 engines, a modification was introduced in the form of a 0·010-in. deep groove surrounding the oil-feed holes in the crankpin journals. More oil is released under pressure by way of the grooves, thus ensuring a larger splash feed to the cylinder bores. The sketch (Fig. 23) shows the position and dimensions of the modification which can be carried out to any twin-cylinder model manufactured in the years 1948/9.

The crankshaft timing-side plain bearing should be checked for wear—clearance when new between shaft and bush being 0·001 in., and permissible wear clearance being 0·003 in.–0·004 in.

Replacement plain bearings are supplied by the makers in a 0·010-in. undersize to allow for boring out to give the correct shaft clearance after fitting, or they can be obtained finished to a size giving 0·002 in.–0·003 in. clearance, which allows for contraction after being pressed into the crankcase.   Always check the bearing for clearance after fitting and ream or lightly hone to give the internal diameter the recommended 0·001 in. clearance.   The crankcase plainbush-type bearing is removed and fitted by the press method only.

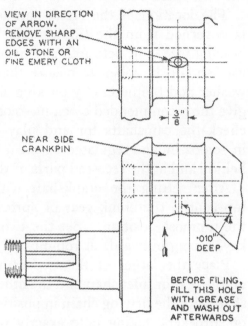

VIEW IN DIRECTION OF ARROW. REMOVE SHARP EDGES WITH AN OIL STONE OR FINE EMERY CLOTH

$\frac{3"}{8}$

NEAR SIDE CRANKPIN

·010" DEEP

BEFORE FILING, FILL THIS HOLE WITH GREASE AND WASH OUT AFTERWARDS

The driving-side roller bearing should be replaced if showing wear, and the outer race can be pressed or drawn out after heating the half-case in boiling water

FIG. 23.—ILLUSTRATION SHOWS POSITION AND DIMENSIONS OF MODIFICATIONS TO OIL-FEED HOLES ON THE CRANKPIN JOURNALS OF 1948–49 MODELS.

or by a light flame application.   The inner race can be driven off the shaft end with a soft punch tool or drift. The replacement inner race must be a tight fit on the shaft, and the bearing outer ring or race pressed into the crankcase housing lip side first.

REASSEMBLING THE ENGINE

Refitting the crankshaft with rods and camshafts is a very simple and straightforward operation, and with all bearings and bushes very carefully checked and renewed as necessary, the work can proceed.

Refitting the Crankshaft and Camshafts

Fit the shafts and bolt up the crankcases, not forgetting the two pinch bolts at the top of the cases.

The location of the crankshaft for end-play clearance is governed from the timing side by the main bush or bearing face, and before finally fitting the crankshaft gear care should be taken to ensure that the hardened thrust washer and the necessary packing shims are in position to give the recommended 0·002 in.–0·004 in. end play. Also check the camshafts for end play—recommended 0·001 in.–0·002 in. and regulated by the use of thin shims placed behind and in the recessed parts of the camshaft sprockets.

After setting the crankshaft with connecting-rods at top centre, the crank gear or sprocket key should be on the topmost position. Set the two camshafts with their keys facing outwards at roughly 45° from the vertical.

Place the larger of the two camshaft-gear assemblies on the rear or inlet shaft and the other on the front exhaust shaft with the driving chain in position over the three gears or sprockets, taking note exactly where the timing dots appear. Turn the crankshaft until the dot on the lower sprocket is at top position and the dots on the camshaft sprockets are almost opposite. The other dots should now be almost at bottom position and under each camshaft centre.

Setting Valve Timing

The above procedure gives an almost direct correct valve-timing setting, but this should be finally checked after fitting the cylinder block and head and with valves and push-rods in position. After the final check and rectifications as necessary, which may mean slightly turning one or both sprockets, they can be finally tightened by driving home on to their respective keyways and fitting end nuts.

The final check must be carried out with the tensioner blade and spring in position and correctly located to give the recommended 0·010 in. clearance between stop and blade end.

Refitting Magneto and Dynamo

The magneto and dynamo both having been very carefully examined and adjusted as necessary (see "Electrical Equipment") should now be refitted to the crankcases. Take note of the type of joint washers required between the magneto and dynamo flanges and the crankcase face, and renew as necessary.

When fitting the dynamo, and engaging the small toothed driven gear with the larger driver, check the clearance between the chain side links and rivets and the face of the small gear. If clearance is nil or close, put two flange washers in position, or better still use a special thick washer which can be obtained from the makers. A distinct metallic knock has been known to be set up in the engine unit due to the timing chain fouling the dynamo-driven gear face, and it is a very important point to watch when reassembling.

The magneto, driving gear and control assembly can next be inserted but should not be finally tightened up until the timing has been set after the cylinder block and pistons have been fitted.

Fitting the Cylinder Block

When fitting the cylinder block use a new base-joint washer in order to prevent oil leakage. The operation is very simple and best carried out with the pistons at lowest position of the stroke. Well smear the bores with clean oil and see that the pistons, rings and clearances are as per makers' specifications (see "Technical Data"). Use new circlips.

Proceed with the fitting of the cylinder-head, etc., as previously mentioned under " Decarbonisation ".

Setting Magneto Timing

Magneto timing can now be set. First, very slowly turn the engine until the pistons are at the top of the stroke and then select the cylinder for timing, which is the one corresponding to the combustion chamber or cylinder-head with both valves closed after the upward compression stroke.

Rotate the engine forward again very slightly and check the piston selected for timing with a thin rule or with a degree chart on the mainshaft until it is set 4° to 8° or $\frac{1}{32}$ in. *after top dead centre.*

Rotate the magneto armature until the metal segment of the slip ring is visible and opposite the high-tension pick-up feeding the sparking plug for the cylinder selected for timing.

Gently rock the armature until the contact-breaker points are just about to open, and in this position very carefully tighten up the armature spindle nut without altering the timing setting.

The timing has been set with the control in the *retarded* position, but it is wise to now check same *fully advanced*. To do this it is necessary to turn by hand the spring-loaded control unit, and when at the full-travel position, which is full advance of the armature, the engine should be gently rotated backwards until the contact-breaker points just break at 30° or ¼ in. *before top dead centre.* This latter timing is recommended as being the one to use for the final setting, especially if any difference should arise between the two movements.

Valve timing should be finally checked before fitting the tensioner blade stop in correct position to give the recommended clearance of 0·010 in. See " Data " for timing chart, and when checking ensure that the rocker or tappet adjustment registers 0·002 in. with engine cold.

Final Assembly

Before reassembling the engine-shaft shock absorber (see page 25) carefully fit the self-aligning rubber and spring-tensioned oil-seal over the driving shaft and against the face of the crankcase; this prevents oil leakage from the case via the roller bearing into the primary chaincase.

Well prime the oil pump with clean oil before reassembling (see pages 63 and 196).

To refit engine unit into the frame reverse the dismantling procedure. Apart from the *engine unit* all information and data for single-cylinder models is applicable to twin-cylinder models.

DATA FOR 1948/51 TWIN-CYLINDER MODELS " KG " AND " KH "

Engine

Cyl. Bore : 63 mm.

Engine Stroke : 80 mm.

Cubic Capacity : 498 c.c.

Compression Ratio :
   Standard L.C. Piston " KG " and " KH ", 6·8–1.
   H.C. Piston " KH " when fitted, 7·5–1.

Peak Revs. :
   " KG ", 6000 r.p.m.
   " KH ", 6500 r.p.m.

B.H.P. :
   " KG ", 24·0.
   " KH ", 26·0.

Valve Timing (with 0·002 in. clearance) :
   Inlet Valves open 15° or $\frac{1}{16}$ in. before T.D.C.
   Inlet Valves close 55° or $\frac{9}{16}$ in. after B.D.C.
   Exhaust Valves open 46° or $\frac{13}{32}$ in. before B.D.C.
   Exhaust Valves close 20° or $\frac{1}{8}$ in. after T.D.C.

Ignition Timing : Piston position before T.D.C., 30° or $\frac{1}{4}$ in., with automatic control in fully advanced position.

Piston Clearance (Standard and High Compression) :
  Ring Land, 0·0198 in.–0·0223 in.
  Below Rings, 0·0048 in.–0·0063 in.
  Extreme Skirt, 0·0028 in.–0·0043 in.
Measurements taken at front and rear piston thrust bearing
  face.   Pistons " ground cam oval ", *i.e.*, 0·010 in. minus at
  gudgeon-pin boss sides.
Piston-rings :
  Compression, 2·4803 in. O/dia. × 0·088 in.–0·094 in. width
    × 0·063 in.–0·064 in. thick.
  Oil Control, 2·4803 in. O/dia. × 0·085 in.–0·091 in. width
    × 0·1245 in.–0·1255 in. thick.
  Gaps, 0·008 in.–0·010 in.
Gudgeon Pin : Outside Diameter, 0·6862 in.–0·6865 in.
S.E. Bush : Reamed after fitting, 0·6863 in.–0·6868 in.
Valves : Stem Diameter.
  Inlet, 0·311 in.–0·312 in.
  Exhaust, 0·309 in.–0·310 in.
Valve Guides : Internal Bore, 0·313 in.–0314 in.
Tappets : Stem Diameter, 0·3415 in.–0·342 in.
Tappet Guides : Internal Bore, 0·3425 in.–0·3435 in.
Rockers : Internal Bore, 0·4995 in.–0·5005 in.
Rocker Spindles : Bearing-Face Diameter, 0·498 in.–0·499 in.
Camshaft Bushes :
  Flanged Type.   Timing Side, 0·874 in.–0·875 in.   Reamed
    after fitting.
  Plain Type.   Drive Side, 0·6255 in.–0·6245 in.   Reamed after
    fitting.
Camshafts :
  Bearing Ends.   Diameters, 0·623 in.–0·624 in. and 0·873 in.–
    0·8735 in.
  End Threads, ⅜ in. × 20 T.P.I.
Crankshaft Bush (*Lined*) : 1·2505 in.–1·2510 in.   Reamed after
  fitting.
Crankshaft :
  Timing Side Bearing End.   Diameter, 1·2495 in.–1·250 in.
  Drive Side Bearing End.   Diameter, 1·125 in.–1·1255 in.
  B.E. Crankpin Journal.   Diameter,1·3745 in.–1·375 in.
  Thread.   Driving End, ¾ in. × 20 T.P.I.
  Thread.   Timing End, ⅜ in. × 20 T.P.I.
Crankcase Roller Bearing : Drive Side, MRJ 1⅛ in. Lipped.
Bush in crankcase for oil-pump driving shaft.   Internal Bore,
  0·3745 in.–0·3755 in.   Reamed after fitting.
Timing Chain : 8 mm. Pitch × 5 mm. Roller × 72 Pitches.
  (Endless.)

CHAPTER V

SINGLE-CYLINDER ENGINE

Simplicity of design and the makers' desire to incorporate the interchangeability of component parts has produced an engine which has a very marked degree of popularity with all Ariel owners. Many parts of the current-type engines allow almost obsolete models to be kept in service if adapted, and it is through this feature that any servicing and maintenance schedules can be applied to every Ariel single-cylinder engine produced since 1933. This text refers mainly to the current-type engine as fitted to all Ariel singles since 1938, when the first totally enclosed cylinder head and rocker boxes were incorporated. The general remarks, however, can be applied to singles of all capacity except where specific points vary.

MAINTENANCE

1938–1951.—All Models 250-c.c., 350-c.c., 500-c.c. O.H.V. and 600-c.c. S.V.

Maintenance adjustments are of the usual type associated with all single-cylinder internal-combustion engines, and confined chiefly to the valve clearances, carburetter, magdyno and lubrication system. Reference to the data chart (p. 109) should be made regarding correct settings for the above, but attention should be given to the lubrication, taking into consideration the conditions under which the assembly is run.

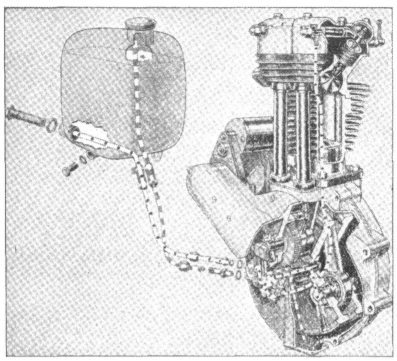

FIG. 24.—LUBRICATION SYSTEM INCORPORATED ON ALL SINGLE-
CYLINDER MODELS (1933–1951).
The white dotted line indicates the delivery line.

Lubrication

The dry-sump system, incorporating a dual plunger oil
pump driven by a small crank extension on the end of
the cam spindle, forces oil direct to the big-end bearing
by way of the flywheel gear-side mainshaft (see Fig. 24
above).

Located in the right-hand or timing-side flywheel is the
oil purifier, which is a tubular reservoir extending from
the big-end to the outer rim of the flywheel where a cupped
plug is fitted.

Due to centrifugal action, all foreign matter in the oil is
passed towards the cupped plug, where it is collected and
retained until the cleaning-out process. It is recom-

mended that this purifier be removed for cleansing every 4000–5000 miles, and is quite accessible after removing the crankcase sump filter or when the cylinder barrel is dismantled for top overhaul.

If difficulty is experienced in removing the purifier plug with an ordinary tube or box spanner, give the hexagon head a hard blow with the hammer, which will have the effect of very slightly stretching and loosening the thread. An inner tube was fitted in the cupped plug on some engines, but this is not now fitted and can always be discarded from former assemblies.

The sump filter should always be washed out whilst removed, and when refitting take care to locate the copper oil-return pipe correctly in the hole provided in the top of filter gauze. Always fit a new joint washer to the sump plate.

The oil-tank filter should be removed and washed out at the same time; when replacing ensure that the internal oil-pipe is located correctly.

Important Note—Oil-pressure Gauge

The oil-pressure gauge fitted to Ariel single-cylinder models, except 1951, does not indicate, and has no effect whatever on, the *amount* of oil pumped into the engine. The actual pump pressure is constant, and the supply of oil will be maintained to the big-end bearing even if no pressure regulator or gauge is fitted, providing, of course, that the delivery side of the pump is in order. Therefore the gauge does keep one informed of the fact that the pump is working, but adjusting the pressure and gauge reading does not vary the main feed supply. On 1938 and subsequent models the adjustable pressure regulator will only vary the amount of oil supplied to the overhead rocker system. Do not adjust to a higher pressure than 10–15 lb. under normal running conditions, because the higher pressure will only increase the load on the delivery pump.

How to Test the Oil Feed—

To test the oil supply from the pump on all models up to 1941 which are fitted with a pressure regulator, remove the plug above this with the engine running, and oil will be pumped out of the plug-hole if the delivery pump is functioning correctly. The 1941 and subsequent single-cylinder engines are not fitted with the pressure regulator, and the oil supply can be tested by detaching the lower end of the oil-pipe to rocker box, and with engine running oil should flow from the union stud.

—and Return

To test the oil return flow with engine running, remove the oil-tank filler cap and ascertain if oil first of all returns in a stream, and then in a regular flow of bubbles only, which is the correct condition of working.

The 1941 and subsequent engines not fitted with the pressure adjustable regulator have incorporated instead a spring-loaded ball valve in the timing cover behind the oil pump. To clean this valve, remove the oil pump and with pliers pull out the steel plug, remove the ball and spring and wash in clean petrol. The plug is grooved on side-valve engines and acts as a pressure release when engine is stopped and assists the zero action of the oil gauge.

Excessive Oil Consumption

This is usually associated with heavy smoke emanating from the exhaust system and may be due to the fact that the return side of the oil pump, fitted with the larger plunger, is not functioning to its full capacity. Foreign matter under the plunger ball valve will cause the pump to fail, and the only remedy is to remove the com-

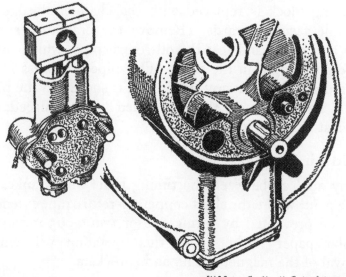

[*"Motor Cycling"* Copyright drawing.

FIG. 25.—OIL PUMP WITH JOINT WASHER AND EXTRA 0·005-IN.
WASHER AT RETURN OIL PIPE JOINT (ALL MODELS 1933–1951).

plete oil pump from the timing-gear case, dismantle and clean.

Access to the pump is by first removing the magneto-chain cover and then the two pump securing screws. Remove both delivery and return base plugs in the pump body and expose the small coil springs and steel $\frac{7}{32}$-in. balls. Thoroughly clean and tap the balls gently into their respective seatings to ensure a good, clean fit. Examine the plungers for wear when fitted, and if excessive play is found renewal of pump body and plungers is advisable. See that the pump body is a good fit on the aluminium face of the gear cover and, if necessary, gently reface by rubbing down on a flat surface plate. Two paper joint washers can be fitted to a pump that is low on the face. Always ensure that the joint washer correctly registers with the holes in the pump and gear cover and that no overlap occurs.

When refitting the oil pump see that the duralumin

operating block is replaced with the chamfered edge of the hole facing inwards.   Remove the crankcase sump plate and gauze and test the oil-return pipe, which must be perfectly tight in the case.   This pipe is a press fit in the housing, but if at any time a leak is suspected the pipe should be withdrawn, thinly " tinned " and replaced, or, better still, renewed.

Avoid Air Leaks

Any air leak between the timing cover and crankcase, at the point where the short copper oil-return pipe extends, must be prevented by fitting one or two 0·005-in. small circular paper washers, but this operation will entail removal of the magneto chain and sprockets.

Breather Valves

Breather valves consisting of elbow unions with a freely rotating steel ball in each have been fitted to all engines with the dry-sump system.   Loss of oil through a breather valve may be caused through inefficiency in the oil return or if the union has not been screwed far enough into the timing-gear cover.   See that the $\frac{1}{4}$-in. ball is in position. On all engines prior to 1941 it is held by a split ring, although free to float.   All elbow unions fitted since 1941 are of the 90° type and only located at the back of the cover, the ball being held in position by a wire pin.

When refilling the *oil-tank*—after washing-out every 1000 miles—do not fill beyond a level of 1 in. below the top of the return pipe and "top up" frequently to maintain this level.

Timing Chain

The magdyno chain should be frequently checked for tension and adjusted to give $\frac{1}{4}$-in. approximately up-and-down lift.   Test for wear, which is indicated by tight and loose positions when engine is rotated, and renew if necessary.

Adjusting Tappets

Tappet or valve-stem clearance should be checked and adjusted every 1000 miles. Correct clearance with engine cold is:

600-c.c. side-valve . Inlet 0·003 in.   Exhaust 0·0c6 in.
All O.H.V. models . Inlet nil.   Exhaust 0·002 in.

When adjusting O.H.V. tappets to clearance as stated, set the piston near T.D.C. with both valves closed and, with the tool-kit spanners provided for this purpose, adjust the rocker-arm adjusters until the valve end caps can be just felt to rotate on the stems.

Side-valve tappets are of the common hexagon-headed type with locknut and present no difficulty with adjustment, which is

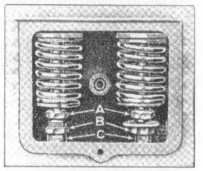

FIG. 26.—METHOD OF ADJUSTING VALVE STEM CLEARANCE—ALL 1936-1951 600-c.c. SIDE-VALVE MODELS.

carried out with the piston at T.D.C. and both valves closed.

Adjusting Exhaust-Valve Lifter

Exhaust-valve lifter adjustment is carried out when valves are closed; with the side-valve model the control cable is adjustable. Leave approximately $\frac{3}{16}$-in. or $\frac{1}{4}$-in. slack movement before the lifter actually commences to operate.

The O.H.V. lifter arm must be adjusted to provide the slack movement, and this arm is fixed on a taper spindle. To loosen arm, undo the securing nut a few turns and with a light hammer give the nut face a sharp tap. Set the arm to the correct angle and re-tighten nut.

The lifter spindle also comprises a small valve head with a seating similar to an engine valve, and if oil leakage is noticed at the spindle hole, remove the complete lifter, dismantle and grind in the valve in the manner of engine valves. Also fit new cork gland-washer if leakage is severe.

"TOP OVERHAUL" AND DECARBONISATION

The average single-cylinder engine in daily service should be regarded as due for " top overhaul " at 3000 to 4000 miles' running. Symptoms indicating this are such as a falling-off in maximum speed and acceleration, loss of compression, undue mechanical noise and possibly excessive oil consumption.

Side-Valve Engine

The side-valve cylinder can be removed without removing the petrol tank, but it is more convenient to dismantle the cylinder head first. Ordinary kit spanners only are required to remove head bolts and base nuts, etc. After detaching the carburetter, exhaust pipe and exhaust-lifter cable, set the piston at B.D.C.—bottom dead centre—lift the cylinder up, tilting forwards and clear of the frame.

Valves, Guides and Seatings

Remove the valves by means of a valve-spring compressor tool, which can be obtained from the makers. The cylinder and cylinder head can best be cleaned of all carbon deposit by immersion in a strong solution of caustic soda. Do not attempt, however, at any time to clean aluminium with this solution, or serious results will ensue.

Check valve guides for wear, and regard them as due

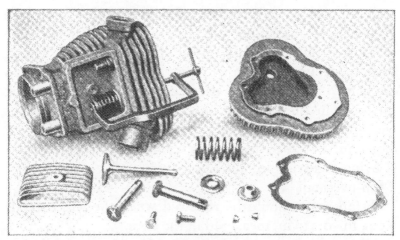

FIG. 27.—CYLINDER AND HEAD ASSEMBLY (1936–1951 600-C.C.
SIDE-VALVE).
Showing method of removing valves.

for replacement if stem clearance of 0·008-in. inlet and
0·010-in. exhaust is exceeded. The side-valve tappet
guides should not need replacement for at least 20,000
miles' service. All valve and tappet guides are a plain
press fit, and can be removed and refitted by using a double-
diameter drift tool.

Examine valve seatings, and if at all pitted or grooved
beyond ordinary regrinding, a seating cutter of 45° should
be lightly applied to recondition them. If valves do not
require refacing they can be ground in to their respective
seatings with the aid of ordinary grinding paste. No
special tool for holding side valves is necessary whilst
grinding. Lightly rub down the top face of cylinder and
cylinder-head base on a flat surface plate, using fine
emery paste or cloth, and prepare the joint gasket if in
good condition for refitting, but renewal is advisable.

The Piston

Removal of piston is carried out by first taking out the
wire circlips retaining the gudgeon-pin. Use a pointed

scribing tool to prise out the clips, and always replace with new if available. Support the piston on one side and drive out the gudgeon-pin from the other with a drift made up from an old pin or steel bar smaller in diameter. Clean piston after removing rings and check for wear in the cylinder bore. Refer to data chart for clearances when new, and if these are exceeded by 0·008 in. or 0·010 in. a new cylinder or reboring and sleeving is advisable, but this is very unlikely at the first " top overhaul ".

Piston-rings should be renewed when the gap exceeds 0·025 in.–0·030 in. measured in the bore.

All Ariel pistons are known as " oval ground ", *i.e.*, 0·010 in. is ground from each gudgeon-pin side of the piston. Therefore, all clearance measurements should be taken at the bearing faces front and rear. One type only of oversize piston is available at the Ariel factory, that of 0·020-in. o/s.

Gudgeon-pin and *small-end bush* clearances should not exceed 0·004 in.–0·005 in. Oversize gudgeon-pins are not supplied by the makers, and when clearance is detected as above, it is advisable to replace the small-end bush. The bush can be removed during the " top overhaul ", but this is best carried out when engine is completely dismantled, as a hand or power press can then be used. To remove bush with flywheels in the crankcase, the draw-bolt-and-collar method can be used, and also for refitting new bush, which should be reamed to suit the gudgeon-pin after fitting. Refer to data chart (p. 111).

Having completed the " top overhaul " bench work, the order of assembly is the reverse of dismantling and, apart from taking care to space correctly the piston-rings with gaps on opposite sides, the whole operation is fairly simple and straightforward.

" Top overhaul " should include some first-aid atten-

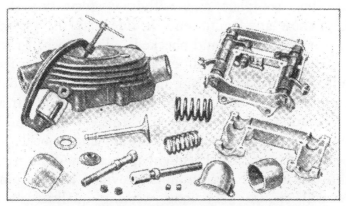

Fig. 28.—Cylinder Head and Rocker Box Assembly
(1936–1937 O.H.V.).
Showing method of removing valves.

tion to the magdyno and carburetter as well as chain and other adjustments, all of which are covered in later chapters.

Although the above text refers to the 1936–1951 600-c.c. side-valve engine, the general principles can be applied to all side-valve units manufactured since 1932 when the detachable cylinder head was first incorporated.

O.H.V. Engine " Top Overhaul "—250-c.c., 350-c.c. and 500-c.c. Models

The 1936–1937 models were fitted with a cast aluminium rocker box carrying the complete rocker gear. This box assembly can be removed from the engine without removing the petrol tank. Decarbonisation and removal of the cylinder barrel are carried out on similar lines to that of the side-valve model, and the same remarks regarding examination of the piston, etc., apply to the complete range of single-cylinder machines.

Removing Rocker Box of 1936–1937 O.H.V. Models

Rotate engine to close both valves and remove the four rocker-plate bolts securing plate to cylinder head. Lift rocker box complete and withdraw sideways. If the rockers show any undue end or side play the assembly should be dismantled and checked. The top half rocker box, when removed, will expose the rocker hardened spindles and distance collars, and, after noting the order of assembly, remove the spindles and check bearing surfaces for size and wear; also rocker arms. Only complete renewal of these parts will eliminate any undue mechanical noise caused by wear. Frequent application of the grease-gun to the special greaser nuts provided in the spindle ends will ensure very long wearing qualities of the assembly.

The grease enters the hollow spindles and also the rocker ball ends where they fit into the top cup of the push-rods. Clean out the complete grease line and hole in the ball end. Note the position of all fibre and rubber oil-retaining washers at the push-rod cover ends and renew the complete set at every " top overhaul ".

Lift out the push-rods and check ball and cup ends for wear, and ensure that these are not loose on the rods.

Removing Rocker Boxes of all 1938–1951 Single-Cylinder Models

It is necessary to remove the petrol tank in order to obtain easy access to the four bolts securing each separate rocker box to the head. Note the long bolt for fitting to the push-rod end of the box. To dismantle the rockers, remove the flat, large-headed screws from the left-hand end of spindles and the dome nuts securing oil-pipe assembly; the rocker spindles can then be pressed or driven out towards the left-hand side. Check position of distance washers, diameter of rocker spindles and bore of rockers. When removing the cylinder head take care not to drop the valve-stem hardened end caps. It is possible for these to pass down the push-rod covers and

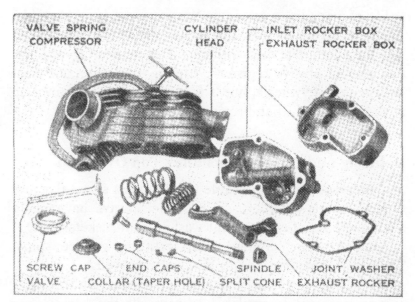

VALVE SPRING COMPRESSOR   CYLINDER HEAD   INLET ROCKER BOX   EXHAUST ROCKER BOX

SCREW CAP   END CAPS   SPINDLE   JOINT WASHER
VALVE   COLLAR (TAPER HOLE)   SPLIT CONE   EXHAUST ROCKER

FIG. 29.—CYLINDER HEAD AND ROCKER BOX ASSEMBLY FOR 1938–1951 SINGLE-CYLINDER O.H.V. MODELS.
Showing method of removing valves.

enter the valve timing chest with serious results if the engine is run later.

Notes on Inspection

Decarbonisation, valve removal and piston examination are similar to the 1936–1937 O.H.V. and side-valve models. Reference should be made to the data table beginning on p. 109 when checking all working parts and bearings.

Do not interchange valves. Note that all inner valve springs are taper formation, the large end fitting next to cylinder head.

During " top overhaul " it is always advisable to check the connecting-rod big-end bearing for direct up-and-down play. After removing the barrel and piston, test the bearing for wear by pulling on the rod with the fly-wheels at the top as well as at the bottom of the stroke.

A lift of 0·004 in.–0·005 in. indicating wear is permissible, but if in excess of this, the engine should be regarded as due for a complete dismantling. The connecting-rod big-end should always register 0·010 in.–0·012 in. side-float between the flywheels, but if ⅛ in. is felt and measured up at the small-end, then bearing wear is indicated.

Refitting and Adjustments after Top Overhaul

General remarks applicable to all models side-valve and O.H.V. single-cylinder. If possible, always have ready a complete set of engine joint washers and gaskets.

Always renew circlips when refitting gudgeon-pins. Fit piston same way round as when removed.

When fitting cylinder barrel single-handed and no ring-compressor tool is available, always tilt the barrel over the piston-ring ends in turn first before attempting to enter the full ring.

To obtain an accurate ignition setting, before fitting the cylinder head, note piston position by placing a steel rule or bar across the top of barrel and measure exact distance B.T.D.C. required according to model.

Ariel single-cylinder models O.H.V. are not fitted with head-joint gaskets. Metal-to-metal system is employed ; the barrel and head should be ground in together by smearing a little valve-grinding compound on the faces and rotating the head on the barrel in the same way as when grinding in a valve.

Always refit the hardened valve end caps to O.H.V. models.

Do not interchange push-rods and ensure that these are located properly in the cam-lever sockets of O.H.V. models.

Adjust tappets with an extra clearance of 0·001 in.– 0·002 in. until valves have properly settled in after grinding and, after a few hundred miles' running, readjust to correct clearance.

Tighten all holding-down bolts and nuts after warming the engine.

COMPLETE CRANKCASE ASSEMBLY OVERHAUL

Removing Engine from Frame as a Complete Assembly, 1936–1951 all Models

The crankcase and primary chain oil-bath layout is common to the complete range of singles, with the exception of the 1939 250-c.c. models " OG " and " OH ". The latter were fitted with a lighter crankcase and oil-bath and a totally enclosed clutch, but apart from these requiring a little difference in method of dismantling, the general principle and covering remarks are applicable.

The petrol tank need not be removed. Dismantle carburetter and all control cables and remove battery and exhaust pipes. Drain and remove the oil-tank complete with two pipes. Detach the foot-rests and rod and take note of the distance piece fitted between the rear engine plates.

Except on the 1939 250-c.c., remove the clutch dome, complete clutch and the outer half of the primary chain-case. Refer to later chapter regarding clutch and gearbox dismantling.

Remove complete engine shock-absorber assembly held in position by two locknuts, and the driving sprocket, together with clutch chain-wheel and primary chain, can be withdrawn from off the shafts. Do not lose the clutch chain-wheel needle rollers.

Remove rear portion of primary chaincase, battery carrier and bolt holding the rear mudguard bracket to engine plate.

Support the engine underneath with suitable packing

and release the gearbox adjuster. Remove the top gearbox fixing-bolt and release the tie-bolts which pass through the engine plates and crankcase lugs. Remove the two bolts holding the front engine plates to the frame as well as the two rear, and the engine unit can be lifted clear of the frame, but complete with rear plates and magdyno mounted on the plate platform.

With the engine securely held in a strong vice by clamping on one of the front crankcase lugs, the cylinder head, rocker boxes and cylinder barrel should be removed as described under " Top Overhaul ".

The Magdyno and Timing Gear is Removed as Follows

Take off oil pump. Place a small steel protector cup over the oil-pump crank drive after removing sprocket securing nuts and, with extractor provided in the tool-kit by makers, pull off both sprockets complete with the endless driving chain. Remove small hexagon bolt holding magneto platform to the chaincase and the three magdyno-base fixing bolts located under the magneto platform.

Take note of the order of assembly of the felt washer and metal retainer at the joint between magdyno end plate and the timing case.

Rear engine plates can now be removed, and the timing-gear cover is ready to be detached by first removing the five securing screws. Whilst pulling the cover away from the crankcase, press on the camwheel spindle to retain the gear in position for checking purposes. Withdraw the camwheel and cam levers and pull off the timing pinion by first removing the securing nut, which has a left-hand thread. Note the small key and keyway in the spindle and pinion. The pinion is a tight fit on the spindle and can only be removed with the kit extractor. Note the correct way for refitting pinion is with the

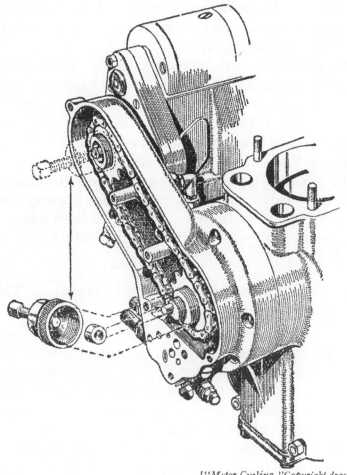

["*Motor Cycling* "*Copyright drawing.*

FIG. 30.—MAGDYNO SPROCKET EXTRACTOR (ALL MODELS
1933–1951).

chamfered side facing inwards. Also note timing dots
on pinion and camwheel, and when these are meshed
together the valve timing is set correctly.

Cam Gear, all Models 1933–1950

Cam levers are fitted with the oil-hole uppermost and
the inlet lever placed in position first. Check faces for
wear and renew if grooved.

Camshaft bushes in timing cover and crankcase should be checked for wear, and if excessive clearance is observed new bushes are advised.

To remove a bush, gently warm up the aluminium cover or crankcase and press out with a suitable double-diameter drift or press tool, taking care to support the centre of the assembly. Press in the bush in the cover with the oil-hole corresponding to that in the cover, and also note that this bush is grooved. The camshaft bush in the crankcase is grooved, but not drilled with an oil-hole.

Refer to data chart relative to sizes for reaming bushes after fitting. Ream bushes together by using a long pilot-type reamer and with the timing cover bolted to the half crankcase.

Cam-Gear Assembly—500-c.c. Model "VH"; 350-c.c. Model "NH" (1951)

The de luxe models 500-c.c. "VG" and 350-c.c. "NG" having been discontinued at the end of the 1950 season, the makers decided to re-design the Red Hunter cam-gear assembly for 1951. The familiar Ariel cam gear used on all Hunter models since 1939, and employing two separate cams machined and ground from the solid bar was superseded by a single wide cam for operating the two cam levers, which were also modified. Unlike the earlier pattern levers, which were identical and inter-changeable for either exhaust or inlet, the 1951 levers consist of a forked-type exhaust and plain-type inlet, the latter being fitted into the fork before being placed on the cam-lever spindle, with the inlet in the rear position nearest the induction.

A slightly different valve timing is obtained by using the 1951 cam assembly (see "Data", page 109).

The gear wheel and small pinion on the flywheel spindle are both marked with timing dots as before, and it is impossible to set the valve timing incorrectly if these dots are intermeshed.

The usual Ariel interchangeability feature permits the modified assembly to be fitted to all single-cylinder O.H.V. models produced since 1936, with one exception, that being the 1949/51 special competition model " VCH " with light-alloy crankcases, etc.

The makers claim that with the 1951 cam assembly a quieter action is obtained, together with a considerable decrease in wear on the cam contours and lever pads.

Taking Apart the Crankcase

Crankcase tie-bolts having been removed, place the assembly on the bench and gently drive the two halves apart by tapping with a mallet or hide hammer inside the cylinder aperture.

Tap out the flywheel assembly, but take note of hardened end-play washers which may be fitted to the mainshafts.

Removing Main Bearings

Crankcase bearings are known as an " interference fit ", and can very easily be removed by warming the crank-case to allow for expansion and then striking each half face downwards on a flat, hard surface.   Remove the securing bearing circlip before attempting to tap out and note position of the distance piece between the two drive-side bearings.   Refer to data chart regarding correct type crankcase bearings and note that model " VH " or Red Hunter is fitted with " roller " bearings extra to the usual " ball " type.   Wash out all bearings in clean petrol and examine carefully the inner and outer races for any signs of pitting or scoring and renew if necessary.   Warm crank-case again around bearing housings before pressing in new races.

Cam Lever Pin fit should be dead tight in crankcase.

Check for wear; see data chart, p. 112. The pin can be removed by warming around the fixing boss and pulling out with suitable grips. Warm crankcase again before fitting new pin.

Overhauling Flywheel Assembly when Taper Crankpin is Fitted

The flywheel assembly incorporating a taper crankpin, common to all Ariel singles except model " VH ", can be dismantled without any very special apparatus and it is only necessary to remove first one of the crankpin nuts, right-hand thread, and if a suitable press is not available, place a hardwood wedge or taper chisel between the flywheels near the crankpin and give same a few sharp blows with the hammer to part the wheels. Check the crankpin centre race for pitting or wear, and if it is necessary to remove the pin from the other flywheel, it can be driven out with an ordinary punch or drift and hammer.

Fitting Oversize Rollers

The big-end bearing, comprising crankpin, outer race—which is a press fit in the connecting-rod—and a double row of hardened steel rollers, is supplied as a complete assembly, and the makers' recommendation is for this always to be renewed as such, and not in separate components. For convenience, however, a set of new rollers only can be fitted, either standard or oversize. Rollers can usually be obtained up to 0·003-in. oversize. If it is possible to micrometer measure the original rollers, note that when new these are size $\frac{1}{4}$ in. $\times$ $\frac{1}{4}$ in. Therefore, if these register 0·002-in. wear, this will permit an up-and-down play in the connecting-rod of a minimum of 0·004 in. If oversize rollers are fitted, ascertain that when the complete bearing is made up, there is at least clearance between two rollers when a feeler gauge is inserted of 0·010-in. thickness. A big-end bearing without this circumference

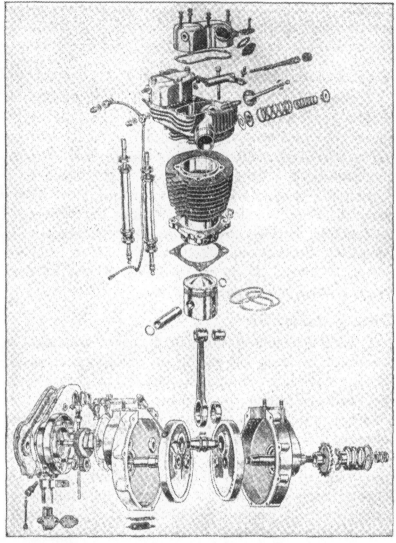

FIG. 31.—EXPLODED VIEW OF THE SINGLE-CYLINDER ENGINE
ASSEMBLY.

Fitted with 1938–1951 type cylinder head and enclosed rocker
assembly.

clearance will give trouble up to a point of serious overheating and subsequent seizure. When refitting a big-
end bearing, check to see that there is a minimum of
0·0005-in. to 0·001-in. maximum up-and-down clearance.

When Parallel Crankpin is Fitted

The model " VH "—500-c.c. Red Hunter—is fitted
with a parallel crankpin of 1-in. diameter (1937–1951)
or of $\frac{15}{16}$-in. diameter (1935–1936), a double row of
rollers which are caged and an outer race pressed into the
connecting-rod. To dismantle the " VH " flywheels it
is advisable to press the crankpin out, but if no press is
available, five or six short bolts and nuts can be inserted
between the flywheels and the nuts unscrewed against one
wheel with the bolts equally spaced.

All " Hunter " flywheels are built of polished steel,
whereas other models are of cast iron.

Testing Mainshafts

Driving-side and timing-side mainshafts should be
tested for wear at the points on which the crankcase
bearings fit. The bearing inner race is a tight push-fit on
the shaft. Examine the driving splines for wear or
fractures and check all threaded portions. If it is found
necessary to replace the shafts, note that for removal the
drive-side is a right-hand thread for the securing nut and
keyed on all models. Timing-side shaft threads are
left-hand either end. The straight crankpin of the 500-c.c
Hunter model is pegged to fit into the drive-side flywheel
and the taper crankpin of all other models is pegged to fit
into the timing-side flywheel.

Most Important

When fitting crankpin to flywheels always check to see
that the oilway extending up the hollow gear-side mainshaft is clear and that the oil-feed hole in crankpin corre-

sponds to the hole in the gear-side flywheel. After fitting
up the complete flywheel assembly, always force oil up the
hollow spindle and check entry of same into the big-end.

Assembling Flywheels

Flywheel alignment after assembly is best carried out
with the use of a special workshop assembling jig. The
common method is to assemble the flywheels and connecting-rod with big-end bearing and before fully tightening
the crankpin nuts to place a straight-edge across the outer
faces of the wheels approximately at right angles to the
crankpin. Tapping the wheels in turn to move same on
the crankpin will bring both more or less in alignment
and the straight-edge test should show this to contact both
flywheels evenly. Then, for a final check before tightening the crankpin nuts, the complete assembly should be
set up between two lathe centres, and if a workshop clock-
dial gauge is available, test each mainshaft for true
running, which should not exceed 0·002-in. error through
mal-alignment.

Refitting Crankcase

The crankcase two halves are machined with a spigot
fixing, and this should be thoroughly cleaned and smeared
with a thin coating of good quality jointing compound
before assembly. Fit flywheels into one half-crankcase
first and then offer up the opposite half. Insert two or
three securing bolts and tighten. Check for end clearance
or " float " in the cases and if this exceeds 0·012 in. dismantle crankcases again and fit on either mainshaft a thin-
gauge hardened end-play washer and re-check. The flywheel assembly must be located centrally in the crankcase
and the end-play washers can be used to determine this.
From 0·008-in. to 0·012-in. end-play is permissible. When
finally tightening up crankcase tie-bolts, see that the top
faces on which the cylinder barrel fits are perfectly even,

no step appearing between the two halves. Any irregularity present at this face will prevent the cylinder from correctly locating, and cause serious mal-alignment and oil leakage.

Reassembling Timing Gears

Refit the timing pinion on the spindle by driving same right home in the keyed position, and when the camwheel is inserted with the timing " dots " corresponding the valve timing is correct. After cam levers have been fitted prepare a new timing cover joint washer to exact pattern, and also the extra 0·005-in. small circular washer for fitting to the short protruding copper oil-return pipe. Before assembling the timing-gear cover see that the oil-feed pipe which passes into the hollow mainshaft is fitted securely in the cover and is not damaged or out of alignment. This pipe is a light driving fit and, as described in a previous page, forms a housing for the pressure ball valve on all 1941 and subsequent models. Refit rear engine plates to crankcase, and bolt down the magdyno on the platform, but leaving the securing bolts for finally tightening after the correct mag. chain tension has been applied. Fit the felt washer and steel retainer to the recess where the magneto armature enters the gear cover, and an extra vellumoid or similar material circular washer over the armature spindle to prevent oil and crankcase pressure entering the magneto gear housing.

Fitting Magneto Drive

Timing-gear cover and chain sprockets with magneto chain in position are refitted and the nut on the camwheel holding the driving sprocket securely tightened. This is best carried out by using a tube spanner and giving the tommy bar a few final hard blows with the hammer. Do not tighten the nut securing the driven sprocket on the magneto spindle, but slide the magneto on the platform to give sufficient pressure to hold the felt washer and retainer and also to obtain correct chain tension. Tighten up magneto base bolts.

Retiming Ignition

Assuming that the piston and cylinder have already been refitted as described under " Top Overhaul ", set the piston at position of degrees before T.D.C. compression stroke with both valves closed, as given in data chart, according to model. Set ignition control to fully advanced position and contact breaker points to just commencing to open. Note that the magneto rotates anti-clockwise from driving end when setting the breaker. With magneto armature and piston in relatively correct positions, place a tube spanner over the armature spindle against the sprocket to clear the nut, and give same a few sharp blows with the hammer to tighten the sprocket on the taper. No key is used on the spindle. Securely tighten spindle nut and re-check the mag. timing.

Refit oil pump after checking as described under " Lubrication " (p. 84), and also deal with adjustments to carburetter and magdyno, etc., as laid down in Chapters VII and XII.

Replacing Engine in the Frame

Engine refitting to the frame is fairly obvious, being the reversal of the procedure laid down for dismantling, but it is necessary to watch carefully the following points :

Ensure that all crankcase tie-bolts and engine plate fixings are dead tight.

Do not omit the foot-rest rod distance piece fitted between the rear engine plates.

See that the shock-absorber assembly is fitted up correctly. The 1941–1951 assembly incorporates an improved type of sliding member and engine sprocket and, as this is interchangeable with all previous types, it is advisable to fit it to any Ariel single-cylinder model whilst in the overhauling stages. Order of assembly is as follows :

(*a*) Plain distance collar next to crankcase bearing ; (*b*) engine driving sprocket ; (*c*) sliding member—no spring cup fitted to 1941–1951 models ; (*d*) shock-absorber spring ; (*e*) spring plate—plain centre hole, not splined ; (*f*) locknut ; (*g*) tab or lock washer ; and (*h*) locknut.

See that a paper joint-washer is fitted at the foot-rest boss between the chaincase halves. This will prevent oil leakage.

The gearbox lower swivel and top clamp bolt must be securely tightened ; also ensure that the flat head of the clamp bolt is located in the D-shaped hole in the near-side rear engine plate.

Final Adjustments

After a complete engine overhaul and attention to the magdyno, carburetter, etc., general adjustments should be made to all controls and driving chains. Run the engine for a short period in order to ascertain that the lubrication system is in order, and carry out the following very useful test to ensure this :

Remove the crankcase sump plate and filter gauze : to the oil-return pipe then exposed, attach a length of rubber tubing terminating in a glass jar containing clean engine oil. With the engine running, the oil-return pump should remove the oil from the jar and pass it into the oil-tank. At the same time, the delivery flow can be tested by detaching the oil pipe to gauge union nut, also by noting the gravity fall of oil from the flywheels through the sump aperture. Refer to previous notes regarding lubrication system and maintenance.

The data tables will be found to contain all useful information relative to the sizes and fits connected with the complete range of Ariel single-cylinder engines produced since 1936. Interchangeability being the predominating feature of Ariel products, it will be noted that many of the foregoing remarks and data items can be applied to early vintage models as far back as 1930.

DATA FOR 1936–1951 SINGLE-CYLINDER MODELS

ENGINE

Model.	Year.	Capacity.	Bore.	Stroke.	Compression Ratio.	Peak Revs.	B.H.P.
		c.c.	mm.	mm.			
VB, Side Valve.	1936–1951	597	86·4	102	5·0—1	4400	15
VG, O.H.V.	1936–1950	497	81·8	95	6·8—1	4600	22
VH (Red Hunter), O.H.V.	1936–1951	497	81·8	95	6·01—1 or 7·5—1 H.C.	H.C. 6000	27
NH (Red Hunter), O.H.V.	1936–1951	348	72	85	6·0—1 or 7·0—1 H.C.	H.C. 5800	17
NG, O.H.V.	1936–1950	348	72	85	6·0—1	5000	13
OH (Red Hunter), O.H.V.	1939 only	249	61	85	7·0—1	6000	13
OG, O.H.V.	1939 only	249	61	85	6·0—1	5400	12
LG, O.H.V.	1936–1938	249	61	85	6·0—1	5400	12
LH (Red Hunter), O.H.V.	1936–1938	249	61	85	7·0—1	6000	13
W/NG (Military Model).	1940–1945	349	72	85	6·5—1	——	——

Note.—Peak revs. on Hunter Models is with H.C. pistons.

VALVE TIMING

Model.	Inlet Opens. Before T.D.C. *	Inlet Closes. After B.D.C. †	Exhaust Opens. Before B.D.C. †	Exhaust Closes. After T.D.C. *
VB.	3/16 in. 22°	1 in. 70°	1 in. 70°	7/32 in. 25°
VG (except 1946–1950).	5/32 in. 5°	11/16 in. 55°	11/16 in. 60°	5/32 in. 20°
VG, 1946–1950.	3/16 in. 22°	11/16 in. 70°	11/16 in. 70°	7/32 in. 25°
VH } all years except NH } 1951.	3/16 in. 22°	11/16 in. 70°	11/16 in. 70°	7/32 in. 25°
VH 1951.	26°	77°	70°	33°
NH 1951.	26°	77°	70°	33°
NG (except 1946–1950).	5/32 in. 5°	11/16 in. 55°	11/16 in. 60°	5/32 in. 20°
NG, 1946–1950.	3/16 in. 22°	11/16 in. 70°	11/16 in. 70°	7/32 in. 25°
LG, LH, 1936–1938.	3/16 in. 22°	11/16 in. 70°	11/16 in. 70°	7/32 in. 25°
OG, 1939 only.	5/32 in. 5°	11/16 in. 55°	11/16 in. 60°	5/32 in. 20°
OH, 1939 only.	3/16 in. 22°	11/16 in. 70°	11/16 in. 70°	7/32 in. 25°
W/NG (Military Model).	5°	55°	60°	20°

* T.D.C. = Top Dead Centre.   † B.D.C. = Bottom Dead Centre.

Note.—Owing to the makers fitting slightly different cam contours at times, variations to the above chart will be found on some models, but if cam gear and timing pinion is meshed to centre-dot markings valve timing will be correct.

IGNITION TIMING

(Piston position before Top Dead Centre. Mag. control fully advanced.)

Model.	Inch.	
VH, NH, LH, OH. (All Red Hunter Models.)	$\frac{5}{8}$.	High speed.
	$\frac{1}{2}$.	Normal touring.
VB 1936–1948 . . .	$\frac{6}{16}$.	
VB 1949–1951 . . .	$\frac{1}{4}$.	
VG, LG, NG, OG . . .	$\begin{cases}\frac{3}{8}. \\ \end{cases}$	$\frac{1}{2}$ with "Hunter" type cam assembly.
W/NG (Military Model) . .	$\frac{1}{2}$.	Before T.D.C.—control fully advanced.

PISTON CLEARANCE

Model.	Below Rings.	Extreme Skirt.
All 250-c.c. . .	0·007 in.–0·008 in.	0·003 in.–0·005 in.
All 350-c.c. . .	0·007 in.–0·009 in.	0·003 in.–0·005 in.
All 500-c.c. . .	0·005 in.–0·007 in.	0·005 in.–0·007 in.

Measurements to be taken at front and rear piston-thrust bearing face. All pistons are "ground cam oval"—*i.e.*, 0·010 in. at gudgeon-pin boss sides.

CAMSHAFT BUSH

All O.H.V. and S.V. . . . Ream after fitting to 0·750-in. diameter.

CAMWHEEL SPINDLE

All O.H.V. and S.V. . . . Diameter ·7485 in.–7480 in.

OIL PUMP

All Models.*	
Delivery plunger . .	Diameter 0·1870 in.–0·1875 in.
Return plunger . .	Diameter 0·3745 in.–0·3750 in.
Delivery pump bore .	Diameter 0·1875 in.–0·1880 in.
Return pump bore . .	Diameter 0·3750 in.–0·3755 in.

* 1950/51 All Models, Delivery plunger, Diameter $\frac{1}{4}$ in.

MAGNETO CHAIN

All Models. . . . $\frac{1}{2}$-in. pitch $\times$ $\frac{1}{8}$-in. $\times$ 35 pitches. Endless type.

ENGINE BALL AND ROLLER BEARINGS

Crankcase ball bearing (except Model "VH").	Size 1 in. $\times$ 2$\frac{1}{2}$ in. $\times$ $\frac{3}{4}$ in. for drive-side.
Crankcase ball bearing (except Model "VH").	Size 1 in. $\times$ 2$\frac{1}{4}$ in. $\times$ $\frac{5}{8}$ in. gear-side and drive-side.

Crankcase ball bearing "VH".	Size 1 in. × $2\frac{1}{4}$ in. × $\frac{5}{8}$ in. drive-side next to roller bearing.
Crankcase roller bearing (Model "VH" only).	Size (lipped) 1 in. × $2\frac{1}{4}$ in. × $\frac{5}{8}$ in. for gear-side.
Crankcase roller bearing ("VH" only).	Size (non-lipped) 1 in. × $2\frac{1}{2}$ in. × $\frac{3}{4}$ in. for drive-side.
Big-end bearing (except Model "VH").	Inclusive *taper* 1 in 6 crankpin. $\frac{1}{4}$ in. × $\frac{1}{4}$ in. rollers. $\frac{3}{4}$ in. × 20 T. crankpin nuts.
Big-end bearing (1935–1936 and part 1937 Model "VH").	$\frac{15}{16}$ in. parallel crankpin. $\frac{1}{4}$ in. × $\frac{1}{4}$ in. rollers in alloy cage. $\frac{3}{4}$ in. × 20 T. crankpin nuts.
Big-end bearing (1937–1951 Model "VH").	1 in. parallel crankpin. $\frac{1}{4}$ in. × $\frac{1}{4}$ in. rollers in alloy cage. $\frac{3}{4}$ in. × 20 T. crankpin nuts.
Crankcase bearing distance collars.	(1) Next to flywheel, 0·165 in. width.
Crankcase bearing distance collars.	(2) Between D.S. bearings except "VH" 0·285 in.
Crankcase bearing distance collars.	(3) Between D.S. bearings "VH" only 0·274 in.
Crankcase bearing and sprocket collar.	(4) Next to sprocket, 0·586 in.

Gudgeon-Pin

All Models.	
O.H.V. and S.V. . .	Diameter 0·8110 in.–0·8115 in.

Small-End Bush

O.H.V. and S.V. . .	*Ream after* fitting to 0·8120 in.–0·8125 in. diameter.

Valves—*Stem Diameter*

Model.	Inlet.	Exhaust.
All 250-c.c. . .	0·311 in.–0·312 in.	0·311 in.–0·312 in. *
All 350-c.c. . .	0·311 in.–0·312 in.	0·340 in.–0·341 in. *
All 500-c.c. O.H.V.	0·342 in.–0·343 in.	0·3695 in.–0·3705 in. *
600-c.c. S.V. .	0·311 in.–0·312 in.	0·311 in.–0·312 in. *

* Valve-seating angle, all models, 45°.

Valve Guides—*Internal Bore*

Model.	Inlet.	Exhaust.
All 250-c.c. . .	0·313 in.–0·314 in.	0·313 in.–0·0314 in.
All 350-c.c. . .	0·313 in.–0·314 in.	0·344 in.–0·345 in.
All 500-c.c. O.H.V.	0·344 in.–0·345 in.	0·374 in.–0·375 in.
600-c.c. S.V. .	0·3135 in.–0·3145 in.	0·3135 in.–0·3145 in.

TAPPET S.V.

600-c.c. S.V.   .   .   . Diameter 0·499 in.–0·500 in.

TAPPET GUIDE S.V.

600-c.c. S.V.   .   .   . Internal Bore 0·5005 in.–0·5015 in.

ROCKER SPINDLE

All O.H.V. 1936–1951   . Diameter 0·498 in.–0·499 in.

ROCKER

All O.H.V. 1936–1951   . Internal Bore 0·500 in.–0·501 in

CAM LEVER PIN

All O.H.V. and S.V. .   . Diameter 0·4890 in.–0·4895 in.

CHAPTER VI

GEARBOX AND CLUTCH ASSEMBLY

THE Burman 4-speed gearbox has been fitted to all Ariel motor cycles since 1931. All models 1936 and subsequent incorporated the foot-change mechanism as standard, although, to special order, a hand-control type can be obtained. The 1949/51 twin-cylinder and the 500-c.c. single-cylinder models, and all four-cylinder 1000-c.c. are fitted with the heavy-weight " BA " type. The 250-c.c., 350-c.c., 1939 600-c.c. four-cylinder models and 1948 twin-cylinder models are fitted with the " CP " type, with one exception, this being the 1939 250-c.c., which is fitted with the Burman " H " light-weight type. The " BA " and " CP " gearboxes are identical in every detail as far as the type of construction is concerned and maintenance and overhaul notes are applicable to both.

Maintenance and Adjustments of the Clutch

All clutch spring adjusting screws should be screwed down only just sufficient to allow the end coil of each spring to be visible when sighted across the face of the centre outer spring plate. Tightening the screws too far will have the effect of compressing the springs beyond a free working limit and will thus render the withdrawal action very stiff and heavy. The correct adjustment is for the spring plate to disengage equally. If the tool-kit special clutch screwdriver is not available, an ordinary driver, wide enough to be filed out U-shape, is suitable for adjustment purposes.

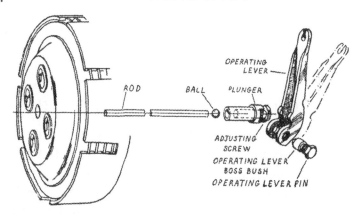

FIG. 32.—CLUTCH WITHDRAWAL ADJUSTMENT.
Fitted with " CP " and " BA " gearboxes on all 1936–1951 models.

The clutch cable adjuster on the top of the kick-starter end-cover should be set to allow the outside operating lever to have sufficient throw or travel, otherwise clutch " drag " and gear " crash " will result.   Adjust the operating lever plunger to give $\frac{1}{64}$-in. clearance between the thrust points.   Frequently check this adjustment by testing the feel of the handle-bar control lever and by pulling and pressing on the operating lever to ensure that no actual direct pressure is applied to the push-rod when the clutch is normally engaged.   Other than an occasional tightening-up of all visible securing bolts and nuts and lubricating the gearbox main assembly and the kick-starter and foot-change mechanism, no other maintenance can be applied.

" Top up " the gearbox occasionally with the makers' recommended brand of grease and also apply the grease-gun to the various nipples if fitted to the kick-starter case and cover.

The gearbox can be considered due for complete dismantling if *gears disengage* whilst under load.   This can be due to a weak pawl spring inside the main casing or to wear on the pawl and ratchet of the foot-change mechanism.   A worn main driving-gear ball bearing, worn driving-gear bushes or operating forks, as well as main pinions worn taper, will all cause gear " jump ".

DISMANTLING COMPLETE GEARBOX

Dismantling is best carried out with the gearbox removed from the frame and securely held in a vice, although it is possible with the box in position to remove the internal gear assembly, with the exception of the main driving-gear ball bearing and driving sprocket.

Removing gearbox from frame of all models 1936–1951 single-cylinder, 1948/51 twin cylinder and all the 1000-c.c., excepting the 1939 250-c.c., is carried out as follows :

Remove Clutch Assembly

Dismantle clutch by first removing the spring-retaining screws with the special kit screwdriver, and the spring plate and all clutch plates, corked or fabric and plain, can be withdrawn. Note order of assembly, the first plate to be fitted being plain, then a fabric or cork plate, then alternate plain plates and, finally, a plain plate before the spring plate carrying spring cups and springs. The mainshaft end nut secures the clutch body and requires removal with a large, heavy-duty type spanner. As the nut is tightened very securely, difficulty may be found in removing this, and if the top gear is engaged and the rear brake applied this will help to keep the shaft from revolving.

An Easily Made Service Tool

A very useful tool for holding the clutch case from turning with the shaft can be made up by obtaining an old clutch plain plate and welding to it a steel flat strip suitably bent to allow the plate to be inserted in the case and the strip portion to engage with the foot-rest or the floor.

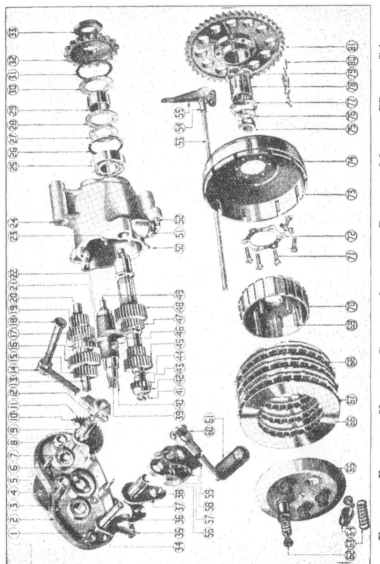

Fig. 33.—Exploded View of Gearbox Assembly—Burman, Models CP and BA. For all Ariel models 1936–1951.

KEY TO FIG. 33

1. Sector spindle bush.
2. Gearbox cover (inner).
3. Camshaft bush (K.S. case).
4. Gearbox cover stud.
5. Layshaft spindle bush.
6. Mainshaft bearing.
7. K.S. spindle bush (inner)
8. K.S. stop peg rubber.
9. K.S. spindle.
10. K.S. quadrant.
11. K.S. spindle.
12. K.S. spindle grease nipple.
13. Layshaft spindle.
14. K.S. lever.
15. Third gear, layshaft.
16. First gear, layshaft.
17. Layshaft clutch.
18. K.S. lever pedal.
19. Second gear, layshaft.
20. Layshaft small gear.
21. Operating fork (layshaft).
22. Operating fork (mainshaft).
23. Gearbox stud.
24. Gearbox shell.
25. Driving gear bearing.
26. Bearing retaining ring.
27. Driving gear inner washer (lipped).
28. Driving gear felt washer.
29. Driving sprocket spacing collar.
30. Driving gear outer washer (flat).
31. Driving gear locating ring (split).
32. Driving sprocket.
33. Driving gear nut.
34. Sector spindle.
35. Gear sector, quadrant and ratchet assembly.
36. Pawl.
37. Control quadrant.
38. Ratchet sleeve.
39. Camshaft rollers.
40. Pinion formed on camshaft.
41. Ratchet nut.
42. Driving ratchet.
43. Ratchet pinion.
44. Ratchet pinion spring.
45. Third gear mainshaft.
46. Operating peg.
47. Mainshaft sliding gear.
48. Driving gear.
49. Camshaft.
50. Gearbox grease nipple.
51. Gearbox filler plug.
52. Gearbox adjustment peg.
53. Clutch operating rod.
54. Clutch operating plunger.
55. Clutch operating lever.
56. Main spring.
57. Pawl spring.
58. Spring box.
59. Cover plate for spring box.
60. Foot control lever.
61. Foot control lever rubber.
62. Clutch spring adjusting nut.
63. Clutch spring.
64. Clutch spring cup.
65. Spring plate.
66. Clutch plain plate.
67. Clutch plate fitted fabric inserts.
68. Fabric insert.
69. Clutch spring stud.
70. Clutch centre.
71. Chain wheel centre bolt.
72. Chain wheel centre tab washer.
73. Clutch case.
74. Clutch-case band.
75. Mainshaft nut, clutch end.
76. Mainshaft nut plain washer.
77. Thrust washer (keyed).
78. Needle roller cage.
79. Thrust washer (plain).
80. Needle roller.
81. Chain wheel.

A heavy blow on the tommy bar of the tube spanner will usually loosen the nut. Many later-type models have a special lock-washer fitted behind the nut. The clutch splined centre can now be pulled off quite easily Examine all splines on which the plain plates slide and remove with a fine file any rough or worn edges. Withdraw the clutch push-rod from the mainshaft and examine for end wear. If the rod is bent or worn it should be renewed, but a temporary repair can be made by building up the end by welding to the correct length and grinding round. The ends are hardened to ensure long wearing.

What to Look for in the Clutch Body

The outer clutch body is next removed by knocking back the ears on the chain-wheel centre tab-washer and unscrewing the six securing pins. Examine the slots in the clutch body and if worn or stepped too badly to reface, the body should be replaced. If any attempt is made to run the motor cycle with the splines, tongues and slots of the clutch assembly worn into grooves or steps, serious sticking of the withdrawal action will take place with resultant gear crashing and " creeping " of the machine.

The Clutch Chain-Wheel

This can only be removed by taking off the outer half of the primary chaincase, detaching the chain and sliding the chain-wheel complete with centre sleeve and hardened needle rollers off the end of the mainshaft. Note that the rollers are not fixed into the cage, and ensure when refitting these that they are kept in position and lubricated by an application of grease.

A plain thrust-washer is fitted behind the needle roller cage and a keyed washer in front with the key portion located in one of the short splines on the end of the main-shaft.

Removing the Gearbox

The gearbox is now ready to be removed from the frame and it is only necessary to take off the oil-tank and battery carrier to give greater accessibility to the top and bottom clamping and swivel bolts. Loosen all rear engine plate bolts and the gearbox adjuster and allow the plates sufficient slackness to enable the gearbox to be lifted out towards the offside.

Clamp the gearbox in a vice by way of the bottom swivel lug and remove the nuts securing the outer end-cover, which can then be pulled away complete with the kick-starter and foot-change mechanism.

Dismantling the Gearbox Internal Mechanism

This operation can now be commenced by unscrewing the hexagon nut on the end of the mainshaft and taking off the kick-starter driving ratchet, ratchet pinion, distance sleeve and short coil spring. These parts require checking for wear, together with the kick-starter quadrant which was removed with the outer end-cover. If the first few teeth of the quadrant are " burred," these should be ground down to give a clean engaging action with the ratchet, but a new part is, of course, advisable.

Remove the inner half gear-cover from the main casing, taking note of the twelve hardened rollers which form the bearing for the gearbox camshaft. Since 1941 many gearboxes have been fitted with a phosphor-bronze bush in place of the roller-type race. Next remove the slotted screwed plug at the base of the main casing and pull out the pawl spring. Pull out the mainshaft from the clutch side and then remove as a complete assembly the layshaft with gears and operating forks.

Inspecting Internals for Wear

Internal pinions and operating forks should be carefully examined, also layshaft spindle and mainshaft. Check for wear on the fork operating faces and renew if at all grooved. Note the order of assembly on the camshaft and that the longer of the two forks is for operating the sliding-gear clutch on the layshaft. Gear pinions very seldom call for replacement, unless through some reason a fractured tooth has occurred. If the gearbox has been long in service it is advisable to check both the layshaft and mainshaft spindles between lathe centres and using a clock-dial gauge. If either shaft shows bending to have taken place and this to exceed 0·005 in., a renewal is advised.

Burman gear pinions are not case-hardened, but being made from oil-toughened nickel-chrome steel, are hard enough to give strength and wearing quality without the risk of frequent fracture, which is more relative to gears which have been case-hardened and treated.

Test the shafts in their respective bearings or bushes and note that a clearance wear of 0·005 in.–0·007 in. is permissible before renewal.

The driving gear and sprocket, having been left in position in the gearbox shell, should be tested for clearance, both internally and externally, and if the centre bushes show a clearance exceeding 0·006 in.–0·007 in. when tested with the mainshaft inserted, fit new ones.

Driving-Gear Bushes

Two are fitted with a centre space for grease deposit between the two and are a tight press fit and require reaming after fitting to give a shaft clearance of at least 0·0015 in.–0·002 in.

To remove the driving gear from the casing the sprocket large locknut must be unscrewed. Some models have a special lock-washer securing the nut, whilst others incorporate the system of punching the inner edge of the nut into one or more of the splines of the driving-gear shank. To hold the gear and sprocket from turning, a very useful tool can be made up and used as follows. Obtain a scrap mainshaft and grind two flats on the thick end which carries the clutch race. Fix this shaft in the vice by gripping the flats. Take the mainshaft sliding gear and place on the splined shaft with the large pinion uppermost. Next invert the gearbox case over the shaft and engage the sliding-gear pinion with the driving gear. The nut can now be unscrewed and the driving gear pushed into the case for removal.

Gearbox Oil Seal

The gearbox manufacturers introduced during the 1948 season a self-adjusting oil-seal to be fitted next to the main driving-gear ball bearing. The idea was to convert the gearbox to " all oil " lubrication ; although the seal was effective in preventing leakage at the bearing end of the box, there was considerable " weepage " elsewhere. With a seal fitted it is advisable to use as a lubricant a fifty-fifty mixture of oil and grease and " top up " with a pressure gun filled with such a mixture.

The oil-seal can be obtained and incorporated on any Burman four-speed gearbox, Type " BA " and Type " CP ". The seal fits, with a thin steel gland washer on either side, immediately behind but after fitting the driving-gear bearing (see Part No. 25, Fig. 33).

Check the Main Ball Bearing and Bushes

The driving-gear ball bearing is easily pressed out of the housing after removal of the circlip and dust-cover. Wash out the bearing and check inner and outer races for pitting and wear. If bearing shows any signs of wear and

" shake " renewal is advised.   A worn bearing will cause gears jumping out as well as undue noise.

The layshaft spindle bush and camshaft bush fitted into the gearbox case should be examined.   These bushes have a flanged-face fitting and are pressed into position. If the camshaft bush flange is worn the shaft can take up a floating action due to excessive end-play, and as the operating forks are located on the shaft this float will readily cause the forks to over-travel with the sliding gears and disengage them whilst under load.

A temporary repair can be effected by placing a hardened shim or washer on the end of the camshaft to compensate for the worn flange, taking care to leave at least 0·001 in.–0·002 in. end-play.

After ensuring that all gear pinions and shafts are in good condition for further service, preparation should be made for reassembling the main gearbox.

Reassembling Gearbox

This is really a reversal of the dismantling operation. Note the correct order of the driving-gear ball bearing, retaining rings, felt washer, etc.   Insert driving gear, fit sprocket and locknut and ensure that this is dead tight. If no special lock-washer is used, it is advisable to lock the sprocket nut in position by centre punching two or three sections of same into the shallow grooves or splines of the driving-gear shank.

Make up into a complete sub-assembly the mainshaft gears, layshaft assembly, camshaft and operating forks, and insert this into the gearbox case, locating the layshaft and camshaft spindles in their respective bushings. Note the position of the camshaft pawl before refitting the pawl spring and plug.   Insert the mainshaft from the driving-side and pass it through the mainshaft sliding gear. Fit on to the shaft end the remaining third mainshaft

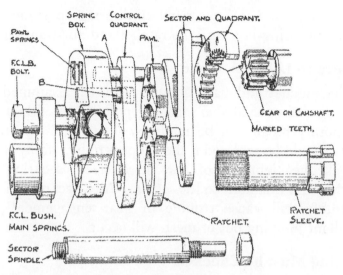

FIG. 34.—EXPLODED VIEW OF THE FOOT GEAR-CHANGE
MECHANISM.

gear. Next place the twelve camshaft hardened rollers
(where fitted) in the shaft groove, which has previously
been well smeared with grease, and fit the gearbox inner
cover, after ensuring the bushes and mainshaft ball
bearing are in good condition. Refit kick-starter ratchet
assembly and tighten mainshaft and nut. Test mainshaft
for end-play which should be $\frac{1}{64}$ in.–$\frac{1}{32}$ in. If end-play
is excessive, this can be reduced by fitting a slightly
longer ratchet pinion steel bush on which the kick-starter
pinion and small coil spring fit. Another method for
reducing end-play is to countersink the inner face of the
shaft nut to allow it to project over the shoulder on the
shaft end and so push the ratchet further along the
shaft.

The foot gear-change mechanism is of the positive type
and allows only one gear at a time to be engaged by one
movement only of the pedal either way. Apart from
accidental damage, the only parts requiring replacement
due to wear and tear over a long period are the two main

coil springs and the two pawl coil springs positioned in the alloy spring-box, and the ratchet and quadrant pawl.

Where to Look for Wear

The ratchet and pawl should be closely examined for any sign of wear at the engaging points and, although a temporary repair can be made by " stoning " up, these parts should be replaced if they appear to be unduly worn. Check the tightness of the three rivets securing the ratchet and quadrant to the sector.   Any slackness of this assembly will cause trouble in gear engagement and resultant jumping out of mesh will occur.

Timing Must be Checked

Note that when actually fitting the foot-change assembly the quadrant and small gear pinion on the camshaft must be correctly " timed " or meshed, otherwise incorrect positioning of gears will result. The quadrant and pinion are marked with distinctive timing dots and these must be intermeshed when the gears are in the neutral position before finally bolting up the outer gearbox end cover.

The Kick-starter

The quadrant and ratchet having been examined or replaced, attention should be given to the kick-starter lever return spring. Ensure that the spring is strong enough to return the lever and pedal to the vertical position after being depressed. A weak spring can have its tension increased by rewinding a further one or two turns. Do not wind the spring up solid, but only sufficient to throw the lever and pedal sharply to the normal vertical position. The inner end of the spring fits into one of the slots on the kick-starter shaft immediately behind the quadrant, and the outer end to a peg provided in the gearbox cover. The correct way for fitting the spring is for it to be located on the shaft with the coils running clockwise from the centre. If fitted the reverse way, the pedal will be thrown to the lowest position instead of to the top of the stroke. The end cover as well as, of course, the main gearbox case should be nearly filled with any of the makers' recommended brands of grease.

Refit the end cover and install the complete gearbox back in the frame. The operation is again simply a reversal of dismantling, and reference should be made to the text describing the clutch assembly before finally replacing the oil-bath chaincase and clutch cover.

Points to watch after a gearbox has been overhauled are chiefly connected with lubrication and clutch adjustment.

Speedometer Drive

Where a speedometer spiral drive is incorporated in the gearbox, ensure that the spirals of the layshaft spindle and the short speedometer drive are kept in good condition by adequate lubrication. It is a good plan to remove the lower end of the speedometer cable and occasionally insert a little thick oil in the spindle housing.

Cork or Fabric Clutch

The gearbox manufacturers recommend that for ordinary touring, traffic work, road and sprint racing, cork is by far the best material, but for grass or sand racing, freak trials and scrambles, fabric is recommended.

Cork possesses greater gripping power and is not affected by oil or water and being slightly elastic takes up the drive in a smooth progressive manner. It will not, however, stand continued slipping as it is liable to burn and char. Fabric does not grip so well as cork and, when fitted, a stronger set of clutch springs must be employed. Fabric will slip if exposed to oil or water and is very fierce on taking up the load due to its hardness and incompressibility.

The 1932–1935 Clutch

This was fitted to the model 4F O.H.C. four-cylinder, last produced in 1936. It is totally enclosed in the primary chaincase and differs slightly from the type previously described, but the method of dismantling is similar. The chain-wheel is fitted with rubber buffers or shock-absorbers and these require renewal periodically.

The clutch centre is a spline fit, but instead of a needle-roller bearing as on the later-type clutches, the chain-wheel centre acts as a bearing outer race for the loose rollers. Any slackness at this bearing should be taken up by fitting a new set of rollers and inner race. See Fig. 33 for order of assembly.

Speedometers

The Smith's speedometers fitted to all Ariel motor cycles are of two types.

Up to 1947, except for a few 1939 " VH " models and the 1940–45 Military W/NG machines, all four-speed models were fitted with a tank-fitting Smith's governor-type instrument with the code letters " PA " on the dial face (" KP " kilos).

All " PA " instruments are gearbox driven, the lay-shaft spindle and the short speedo spindle being suitably geared to give a certain flexible cable drive to which the speedo instrument is calibrated. The " flex speed " for " PA " instruments is 2240.

Chronometric type instruments—usually front fork mounted and gearbox driven—have a " flex speed " of 1610 and, therefore, are definitely not interchangeable with the panel type " PA ". The chronometric speedo gearing—layshaft spindle and short speedo spindle—are machined to give the different ratio required.

DATA ON THE GEARBOX AND CLUTCH ASSEMBLY—BURMAN TYPE

Motor Cycle Model.	Gearbox Type.	Clutch Type.	Clutch Chain-wheel.	Driving Sprocket.
1936. 4-Cyl. O.H.C.	"BA1"	4 cork plates 5 plain plates Totally enclosed	½ in. × 0·305 in. 44T.	⅝ in. × ⅜ in. 19T.
1936 to 1951. Single-cyl. 250-c.c. and 350-c.c., except 1939 250-c.c.	"CP1"	2 cork plates 3 plain plates Needle roller	½ in. × 0·305 in. 44T.	⅝ in. × ⅜ in. 18T.
1948. Twin-cyl. with 3 cork 4 plain.	"CP1"	3 cork plates 4 plain plates	½ in. × 0·305 in. 44 T.	⅝ in. × ⅜ in. 18T.
1936 to 1951. Single-cyl. 500-c.c. O.H.V. and 600-c.c. S.V. 1949–51 Twin-cyl.	"BA1"	3 cork plates 4 plain plates Needle roller	½ in. × 0·305 in. 44T.	⅝ in. × ⅜ in. 19T.
1937 to 1951. 4-Cyl. 1000-c.c.	"BA2"	3 cork plates 4 plain plates	½ in. × 0·305 in. 44T.	⅝ in. × ⅜ in. 19T.
1939. 4-Cyl. 600-c.c.	"CP2"	3 cork plates 4 plain plates	½ in. × 0·305 in. 44T.	⅝ in. × ⅜ in. 16T.

GEAR RATIOS

Model.	Engine Driving Sprocket.		Top Gear.	3rd.	2nd.	1st.
1936. 4-Cyl.	Solo	21T.	5·2—1	6·5—1	8·6—1	13·9—1
Do.	Side-car	19T.	5·7	7·2	9·7	15·3
1936 to 1951. 250-c.c. and 350-c.c., except 1939 250-c.c.	Solo	20T.	5·7	7·3	10·1	15·3
		19T.	6·0	7·7	10·6	16·1
		18T.	6·4	8·2	11·2	17·0
		17T.	6·8	8·7	11·9	18·0
1936 to 1951. 500-c.c. O.H.V. and 600-c.c. S.V.	Solo	23T.	4·7	6·0	8·0	12·6
		21T.	5·2	6·5	8·6	13·9
	Side-car and optionals	20T.	5·4	6·8	8·8	14·5
		19T.	5·7	7·2	9·7	15·3
		18T.	6·0	7·6	10·0	16·2
		17T.	6·4	8·0	10·6	17·2
1937 to 1951. 1000-c.c. 4-cyl.	Solo	25T.	4·3	5·5	7·4	11·6
		24T.	4·5	5·7	7·7	12·1
		23T.	4·7	6·0	8·0	12·6
	Side-car	22T.	4·9	6·2	8·4	13·2
1939. 600-c.c. 4-cyl.	Solo	24T.	5·4	6·9	9·5	14·4
		23T.	5·6	7·2	9·9	15·0
	Side-car	22T.	5·9	7·5	10·3	15·7
1948. Twin-cyl. KG and KH.	Solo	23T.	5·0	6·4	8·8	13·3
	Side-car	19T.	6·0	7·7	10·6	16·1
1949 to 1951. KG and KH.	Solo	21T.	5·20	6·65	9·15	13·85
	Side-car	19T.	5·75	7·40	10·15	15·40

BALL BEARINGS

All Years.	Mainshaft Ball Bearing.	Driving Gear Ball Bearing.
Type " BA " Gearbox.	Size 52 mm. × 20 mm. × 15 mm.	Size 72 mm. × 1½ in. × 17 mm.
Type " CP " Gearbox.	Size 40 mm. × 17 mm. × 12 mm.	Size 62 mm. × 1$\frac{9}{16}$ in. × 16 mm.

CHAINS

Primary Chain Adjustment.—Slacken off pivot and clamp bolts, and rotate nut on draw bolt to swing box about pivot bolt. Adjust until chain has approx. ⅜ in. up-and-down movement midway between sprockets at tightest point.

Rear Chain Adjustment (Rigid Frame, Fixed Rear Wheel).—Slacken off two rear wheel spindle nuts and loosen nut securing brake anchor bar to brake plate ; then adjust by turning screw adjusters by an equal amount. Chain movement, approx. ⅜ in. Adjust rear brake if necessary.

Rear Chain Adjustment (Spring Frame with Fixed Rear Wheel) 1936–39.—Slacken off two hub spindle nuts and rotate adjusting cams in required direction. Each side of wheel must be equally adjusted to ensure correct alignment. 1950/51 Models have Adjuster Bolts and Lock Nuts, see " Spring Frame ", page 168.

Rear Chain Adjustment (Spring Frame with Detachable Rear Wheel) 1936–39.—Slacken off spindle nut on brake side and sleeve nut on offside. Sleeve nut is centre hexagon, inner hexagon being adjusting cam. 1950/51 Models have Adjuster Bolts and Lock Nuts, see " Spring Frame ", page 168.

Rear Chain Lubrication is by means of needle valve in primary chaincase (just behind clutch dome) ; this controls overflow to rear chain. Obtain correct setting by trial on road ; turn clockwise to decrease supply.

Driving Chain Wear.—A permissible stretch of ⅛ in. per foot of chain is allowed before replacement is considered necessary.

CHAPTER VII

CARBURETTER

THE needle jet type carburetter ("Amal") is fitted to all Ariel single-cylinder and twin-cylinder engines and reference should be made to the data chart in this chapter regarding the different models for relatively different cubic capacity engines.

Maintenance of the carburetter is normally confined to detaching and washing out the float chamber, checking and tightening the fixing flange, top and bottom mixing chamber ring and nut and periodically making pilot and throttle stop adjustments.

Adjustments and Tuning—" Amal " Carburetter

The Pilot Air Screw.—If screwed in clockwise this reduces the air supply and richens the slow-running mixture ; turning anti-clockwise weakens the mixture.

The Throttle Stop Screw.—This screw should be so set as to just open the throttle valve sufficiently to keep the engine running slowly with the control lever in the fully closed position.

Regulate the pilot screw and throttle stop so as to enable the engine to " tick over " with an even beat. Too rich a mixture will cause erratic running and a very weak mixture will cause " spitting back " or even failure to run at all. Slow running adjustment is a question of trial and error and experiments must be made with the settings in conjunction with the ignition control lever in various positions.

The Throttle Valve.—The cut-away of the valve or slide

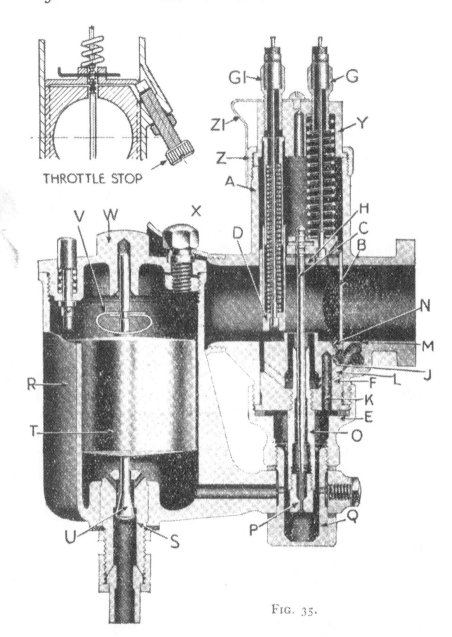

THROTTLE STOP

Fig. 35.

FIG. 35 (*Opposite*).—SECTIONED ILLUSTRATION OF THE "AMAL" NEEDLE JET CARBURETTER, FOR SINGLE- AND TWIN-CYLINDER MODELS.

Air and throttle valves are in the closed position.

A. Mixing chamber.
B. Throttle valve.
C. Throttle needle.
D. Air Valve.
E. Mixing chamber union nut.
F. Jet block.
H. Jet block barrel.
J. Pilot hole.
K. Pilot feed hole.
L. Pilot air hole.
M. Pilot outlet.

N. By-pass.
O. Needle jet.
P. Main jet.
Q. Holding bolt.
R. Float chamber.
S. Needle seating.
T. Float.
U. Needle valve.
V. Spring clip.
W. Float chamber top.
X. Float chamber lock screw.

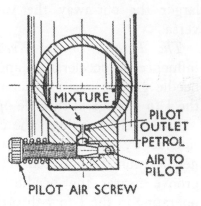

FIG. 36.—SHOWING SIDE VIEW OF THE AIR INLET (SEE FACING PAGE).

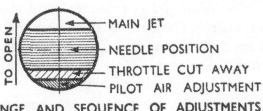

FIG. 37.—SHOWING THE RANGE AND SEQUENCE OF ADJUSTMENTS OF THE "AMAL" CARBURETTER.

controls the mixture between $\frac{1}{8}$ and $\frac{1}{4}$ throttle position. Throttle valves are usually supplied in $\frac{3}{16}$-in., $\frac{4}{16}$-in. and $\frac{5}{16}$-in. cut-away sizes.   The size is stamped on the top face and includes the type of carburetter for the valve to be fitted to.   For example, a 29/3 valve has a $\frac{3}{16}$-in. cut-away and is intended for the "Amal" type 29 carburetter; a 29/4 valve has a $\frac{4}{16}$-in. cut-away and is also intended for the type 29 carburetter, whereas a 6/4 is for fitting to a type 6 carburetter and has a $\frac{4}{16}$-in. cut-away.

Acceleration is governed by the cut-away to a very marked degree, especially when opening up from a partially closed or closed throttle position.   The larger the cut-away the weaker the mixture and vice versa.

The Throttle or Jet Needle also has a considerable influence on acceleration and petrol consumption.   The needle groove position determines the mixture through the $\frac{1}{4}$ to $\frac{3}{4}$ range of throttle opening.

Fitting the needle in the centre groove gives a general satisfactory setting, but if a weaker mixture is desired, the needle must be lowered by fitting the fixing clip in a groove nearer the needle top.   A richer mixture for operating in the $\frac{1}{4}$ to $\frac{3}{4}$ throttle range is obtained by using a lower groove for needle fixing.

The Main Jet is calibrated and stamped with its size number.   The smaller the number the weaker the mixture and vice versa.   The main jet does not normally vary the mixture below the $\frac{3}{4}$ throttle opening unless the needle jet is considerably worn.

Trial and error experiments again are necessary when fitting different sizes of main jets, but, generally speaking, the jet size should be that to produce maximum power and speed with the throttle and the air valve fully opened.

CARBURETTER DATA

Ariel Model.	Year.	"Amal" Type.	Main Jet Size.	Throttle Valve Size.	Float Chamber Type.
4/F "LG" "LH"	1933/6 1936 to 1938	/04 75/014	90 110	4/4 5/4	Level 14°
"VB"	1936 to 1951	76/112	160	6/4	14°
"VG"	1936 to 1950	76/024	170	6/4	14°
"NG"	1936 to 1950	75/014	110	5/4	14°
"NH"	1936 to 1951	76/014	150	6/4	14°
"VH"	1936 to 1951	89/014	200	29/3–4	14°
"KG"	1948 to 1951	276EF	140	6/3	14°
"KH"	1948 to 1951	276EG	150	6/3	14°
"OG" "OH"	1939 only	75/014	110	5/3	14°

Reconditioning the "Amal" Carburetter

Under normal running conditions a carburetter should not require replacement parts under 15,000 miles, although running through dusty or sandy districts may somewhat shorten the useful life of the throttle valve.

Examine and check carefully the actual bearing surfaces of the valve and inside the mixing chamber or carburetter body, and if a slack fit or signs of wear or scoring are present, replacement of both parts is advisable.

The jet block should be removed from the main body and also renewed if the valve sliding guides show wear having taken place.

If the block is tight in position, this can very easily be driven out after slightly warming in hot water. Do not apply direct heat from a flame to any part of the carburetter or the metal alloy may distort.

The needle jet should be replaced periodically, because friction wear over a long period does take place with this part.

Air Leaks

The carburetter body fixing flange should be tested to ensure that no air leakage is present and the flange face should be ground flat on a surface plate, using a sheet of very fine emery cloth or paste.

If a flange is only slightly concave and is bolted up tight to the cylinder or head, there is considerable risk of the mixing chamber or body becoming distorted, with resultant throttle valve sticking in the guides.

Flooding

Always fit a new set of fibre joint washers to ensure fuel-tight joints, and also to maintain correct level of the float chamber in relation to the main jet.   Flooding is generally due to a leaky float or worn float needle and seating.   Top and bottom feed float chambers are fitted to various Ariel models, but the action and construction are similar and apply to each model.

Grinding in the needle taper to its seating is not recommended, but to obtain a perfect seating when a new float needle is to be fitted, the needle can be lightly tapped into its seating by using a soft brass or copper punch and hammer.   Test the float for leaks by shaking and if petrol has entered same, replace if possible.

A temporary repair can be carried out by first ascertaining where the leak is by immersion in water and then piercing another very small hole to act as a vent to empty the float.   A small portion of flux and solder will re-seal the holes.

Enthusiastic riders in search of maximum power and
speeds are advised to obtain from the carburetter makers
a small range of main jets and throttle valves and carry
out experiments and test runs over a selected route.

" Solex " Carburetter

The " Solex " carburetter is fitted to the 1937–1951
1000-c.c. Square Four Models and also to the 1939
600-c.c.

Type " FH " (600-c.c. 1939) with Air Strangler Handlebar
Control.

Standard settings are :—

Choke Tube	.	. 20
Main Jet	.	. 100 × 58
Auxiliary Jet	.	. 55
Jet Cap	.	. 19 × 2 × 140

Type " FH " (1000-c.c. all 1937 and early 1938 engine nos. up
to *DD.* 858).

Choke Tube	.	. 23
Main Jet	.	. 115 × 58
Auxiliary Jet	.	. 055
Jet Cap	.	. 19 × 2 × 140

Type " 26.AH " (1000-c.c. 1938–40, 1946–51 " *Bi- Starter*").

Choke Tube	. 23
Main Jet	. 120
Auxiliary Jet	. 70
Air Correction Jet	. 150
Bi-Starter (Starter Jet)	. 100
Bi-Starter (Air Jet)	. 30

Air Strangler Type

The slow running adjustment is carried out by turning
the screw which is spring loaded on the throttle lever of
the carburetter and should be set for " tick-over " commencing with the throttle control closed.

The slow running mixture is regulated with the other
spring-loaded screw situated near the carburetter fixing
flange. Turning this screw clockwise weakens the mix-

ture and anti-clockwise gives a rich slow running mixture.
Correct position can only be determined by trial and error
in the attempt to obtain a smooth running engine.   The
standard settings can be altered to suit climatic conditions
and altitudes.   If it is desired to improve petrol consumption a size smaller main and auxiliary jet can be tried.
The main jet first number indicates the actual jet hole
calibration and the second number refers to the correction
holes.   Alternative main jet sizes are variable in numbers
of five.   For example—100 × 5, 115 × 58, 110 × 58.

Bi-Starter Type

Slow running adjustment is the same as for the air
strangler type carburetter.

Different sizes of main, auxiliary and air correction
jets can be experimented with and a No. 65 auxiliary
jet will probably improve fuel consumption without
sacrificing performance.   The main jet controls mixture
at cruising speeds and acceleration and a No. 115 or 110
can be tried relative to consumption of fuel.

The Air Correction Jet

Compensates the higher speed mixture.   To weaken
this mixture a larger correction jet is fitted and vice versa.
Therefore, if a smaller main jet is fitted it will probably be
found necessary to fit a smaller correction jet to balance
the mixture at higher speeds.

Apart from the removal of the complete carburetter for
cleaning purposes the only points to watch, in order to
maintain efficiency, are those connected with the fixing
flange and the throttle butterfly.   The fixing flange should
be occasionally tested for air leaks by holding the face
against a flat surface plate covered with fine emery cloth
or paste and lightly rubbing to ascertain if any distortion
has occurred.   Rectify, if necessary, by further refacing

and ensure the fitting of a new joint washer. The throttle valve or butterfly, together with its spindle, should be examined for wear and renewed if necessary.

High-Altitude Setting

In certain countries where a Solex carburetter operates at 3,000 feet and over above sea-level, it will be necessary to employ a different jet setting to that of our British standard.

It is only by a trial-and-error system that a satisfactory combination of jets can be arrived at, but the makers have a general recommendation, which is to reduce the main jet a half size for 3,000 feet, with a maximum reduction of one size for altitudes over 6,000 feet.

The higher the altitude the smaller the main jet is the ruling, and it may be necessary to increase the size of the air-correction jet, but to reduce the auxiliary jet.

CHAPTER VIII

FRONT FORKS AND STEERING ASSEMBLY

THE girder type of assembly was common to all Ariel models since 1934 and, with the exception of the auxiliary side springs which were first incorporated in 1939, is entirely interchangeable throughout the range of various models 1934–1946.

Maintenance consists only of fork spindle and steering head adjustment and lubrication as is described in the following. The telescopic forks with hydraulic control were first introduced and fitted to all models as a standard fitment for 1947 and have remained the standard fitment since that date.

GIRDER TYPE

Fork Link and Spindle Adjustment

Whether it is a matter of routine adjustment or of reassembly after dismantling, correct link and spindle adjustment is most important, and is carried out as follows :

To adjust the fork spindles, slacken the two hexagon locknuts—one at each end of the spindle—and rotate the spindle by means of a spanner placed on the squared end. Rotate anti-clockwise to tighten and clockwise to loosen. Note carefully that re-tightening the locknut at the end of the spindle which is not squared will tighten up the adjustment. Therefore, adjust a little at a time, tighten locknut and test. When the final adjustment has been made, secure the locknut at the squared end.

The reason why tightening the locknut affects the

adjustment is that the spindle at this end is stepped, the shoulder bearing up against the inner face of the link. When the locknut is loosened, the link may move away from the shoulder on the spindle and extra clearance therefore develops.

For correct fork spindle adjustment, the knurled washers next to the side links should just rotate easily.

The fork dampers are adjusted by means of the nut on the right side lower front spindle only.   Keep the spindle screwed right home in the nearside link and the locknut tight.   The star-washer behind the adjusting nut applies the pressure ; the other star-washer is simply a dummy.

For the best results, the forks should have a free action, with just sufficient damping to prevent excessive fork bounce on bad roads.

Lubrication

Lubricate the fork spindles and lower joint pins of the auxiliary damper springs, if fitted, every 500 miles.   Also put a spot of oil where the top anchorages of the auxiliary springs pivot on the fork spindle.

Steering Head

The head bearings are of the cup-and-cone ball type and should be adjusted after the first few hundred miles' running, after which they will require only infrequent attention.

When adjusting the head bearings it is advisable to take the weight off the front wheel by putting a block under the crankcase ; also slacken the steering damper right out.   Now loosen the bolt through the ball head-clip.   Above the clip are two thin nuts ; slacken off the top one—a locknut—and adjust by means of the lower one. The steering should be quite free, but there should be no shake in the handlebars.   Carefully re-lock.

If the ball races are dismantled, note that there must be

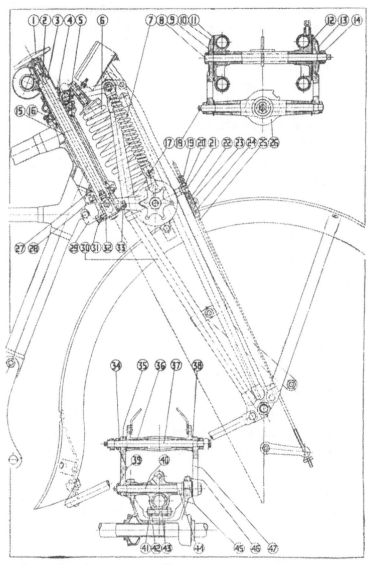

FIG. 38.—GIRDER TYPE FRONT FORK AND STEERING HEAD
ASSEMBLY (ALL MODELS FROM 1936–1946).

KEY TO FIG. 38

1, 2, 3. Steering damper knob, tie bolt and collar.
4. Nut for steering column.
5. Main spring anchorage set pin.
6. Main spring.
7. Auxiliary spring.
8. Link spindle—lower front.
9. Damper star washer—dummy.
10. Middle link, l/s.
11. Damper friction disc.
12. Middle link, r/s.
13, 14. Damper star washer and adjusting nut.
15. Steering column.
16. Dust cover.
17. Auxiliary spring bottom bracket joint pin.
18. Link spindle, lower rear.
19, 20, 21. Brake cable adjuster, locknut and stop lug.
22. Spring box.
23. Spring for connection.
24. Brake rod cable connection.
25. Front brake rod.
26. Steering crown.
27. Felt washer.
28. Steel balls.
29. Steering damper anchor plate.
30. Fork girder.
31. Friction discs.
32, 33. Damper star washer and bottom plate.
34. Top spindle washer, l/s.
35. Top link, l/s.
36. Link spindle bush.
37. Link spindle, top front.
38. Knurled washer.
39. Link spindle nuts.
40. Link spindle, top rear.
41, 42, 43. Ball head clip bolt, nut and washers.
44. Ball head clip.
45, 46. Handlebar bracket and bolt.
47. Top link, r/s.

twenty balls only in each race. It will be found that twenty-one balls can be inserted, but this number makes the steering tight.

Two grease-gun nipples are provided for the two head bearings. Grease here every 1000 miles.

Handlebar Mounting

The handlebar is carried in a bracket in which it is fixed through the medium of compressed rubber rings. The two large compression nuts must always be kept screwed up hard in order that the resilient mounting may work effectively. The small grub screw in the handlebar, behind the bracket, is a safety device to prevent the handlebars turning round, should they not be properly tight in the rubber mounting.

Since 1941, the flexible rubber mounting has been dispensed with on all models, the handlebar being carried in brackets rigidly attached to the ball head-clip.

Removal of a Complete Assembly as a Unit

1. Support the machine by a box under the crankcase and take out front wheel.

2. Remove speedometer and cable if front fixing.

3. Disconnect wiring to headlamp by removing switch panel (held by three screws) from lamp, and take off lamp. Unscrew steering damper knob. Undo the four set bolts clamping the handlebar bracket to the ball head-clip. This will avoid disturbing the controls unless it is required to remove the handlebars, in which case the controls should be uncoupled before undoing the handle-bar bracket. In either case, disconnect the front brake cable at the stop on the forks.

4. Remove the bolt securing the top spring anchorage to the ball head-clip and remove the auxiliary spring top brackets from the spindle. Undo the two thin nuts on the steering column above the ball head-clip, and loosen the pinch bolt through the clip.

5. Remove the small bolt connecting the steering damper anchor-plate to the frame. Undo the two top fork spindle locknuts on the off side, tap this link off the spindles and pull out the nearside link complete with both spindles towards the near side.

6. Force the steering column down through the ball head-clip by tapping gently on top of the column with a mallet. Do not lose the steel balls out of the head-lug ball races as the steering assembly drops out of the frame.

There are twenty balls in each race.

Dismantling Assembly

The offside bottom link is removed in the same way as the top link, after which the nearside bottom link and spindles can be withdrawn as a unit. All four spindles

are screwed into the nearside links and can be screwed out
after removal of the locking nuts.

The hardened fork spindles are carried in porous self-
lubricating composition bushes in the fork girder, ball
head-clip and steering crown.   The bushes can be driven
out for replacement when worn.   When fitting new bushes
force in squarely under a press, if possible.   If no press
is available and the bushes have to be driven in, use
considerable care, as the bushes are brittle and will easily
break.   Try to obtain a shouldered drift which is a fairly
close fit in the bush.   Examine the spindles for wear and
replace if necessary ;   diameter (new) is 0·498 in.–0·499 in.
If new spindles and bushes are fitted, try the spindles in
the bushes before reaming.   If the spindles will not slide
easily through both bushes, ream the bushes to 0·500 in.–
0·501 in. dia.

Removing Fork Girder Only

Disconnect the speedometer, headlamp and springs, and
then take out the fork spindles as described in para. 5 on
page 142 and under "Dismantling Assembly" above.   This
will leave the steering column assembly in the head lug.

Dismantling Steering Damper

To dismantle the damper, support the front wheel off
the ground by means of a box under the engine.   Unscrew
the damper knob and remove the anchor-plate bolt and star-
washer fixing nut.   To take out the tie-rod, which passes
through the column, remove the lower rear fork spindle.

When reassembling note that the nut securing the star-
washer screws up to a small shoulder, leaving the star-
washer free to rotate ;   take care not to trap the washer.
The fixed anchor plate is in the centre of the assembly, the
lipped plate, which rotates with the crown, coming next
to the star-washer.

Fork Girder Repair

If a girder is sufficiently damaged to warrant resetting, this can be carried out " cold ", providing the tubes are not excessively bent. All tube joints are brazed and welding should not be attempted. Red heat can be applied to a bent tube for resetting purposes with no ill-effect to the metal. Suitable leverage adapted with the girder held firmly in a vice is necessary to straighten it and a check must be made for alignment by inserting steel rods through the top- and centre-link spindle holes, as well as one in the hub-spindle fork ends. The three rods should lie perfectly parallel to indicate vertical alignment, but a further check is necessary to ensure perfect side setting. This consists of measuring for equal distances between a line extending from the fork damper face and the forked end on either side. The Ariel factory fork building jigs are used for service repair work and it is advisable to send a badly bent girder to the makers for attention.

Front Fork Main Springs

These should be replaced when weakened sufficiently to allow the top links to ride above the horizontal position. Springs can be removed and refitted by punching the end of the spiral with an old blunt chisel or similar tool. Extra strong springs are obtainable and advisable when a side-car is fitted, but no alteration is necessary to the length of top links, which are standard throughout the Ariel range.

GIRDER TYPE FORK AND STEERING ASSEMBLY DATA

Fork Spindles . . .	0·498 in.–0·499 in. diameter.
Spindle Bushes—Ream after fitting to . . .	0·500 in.–0·501 in. diameter.

Main Spring
  Single-cylinder models—
    Solo   .   .   .   . 0·312 in. wire.
    Side-car .   .   .   . 0·344 in. wire.
  Four-cylinder models—
    Solo   .   .   .   . 0·344 in. wire.
    Side-car .   .   .   . 0·375 in. wire.
Steering-head Steel Balls
  20 Top   .   .   .   . ¼ in. diameter.
  20 Bottom .   .   .   . ¼ in. diameter.
Top Fork Links—centres   . 3¼ in.
Middle Links—centres   .   . 3⁹⁄₁₆ in.

TELESCOPIC FRONT FORK WITH HYDRAULIC CONTROL

The telescopic fork assembly was first fitted as standard to all 1947 Ariels. With the fork a new design of front hub, mudguard top-stay and handlebar is incorporated.

The complete assembly can be fitted—when obtainable from the makers as a separate conversion set—to all machines, single-cylinder and Square Four, without any difficulty. If the assembly has a tendency to foul the forward portion of the petrol-tank with the steering at full lock, and this is possible with models produced previous to 1947, the tank can be moved back slightly by slotting the holes in the tank lugs of the frame.

Maintenance and Adjustments

For the fork, this is solely confined to a periodical tightening up of all nuts and bolts. Once the fork tubes have been filled with oil no further lubrication is necessary. Approximately one-third of a pint of oil of the recommended grade is sufficient for each fork leg and no " topping up " is required. To test the correct oil-level with the machine unladen in a perfectly upright position, remove the two top plated hexagon plugs and insert a dip stick. The level should be 17–18 in. below the top face of the handlebar bracket for all normal running, but if it is desired to improve the damping effect after fitting a heavy type side-car, or for competition work, a higher level can be used.   It is even permissible to use a heavy grade lubricating oil for rough road and " scrambles," but trial and error will determine what suits the individual rider and conditions.

Auxiliary coil springs are fitted to each fork leg and are supplied in two grades—light for solo use and heavy for side-car work.

Exchanging springs may be carried out without any special tools, except for the use of the hexagon socket key supplied by the makers in the tool-kit.   Proceed as follows.   Place a support under the engine to allow the wheel to clear the ground sufficiently and remove the front stand, mudguard and wheel.   Remove the two top plated plugs and loosen the sunken hexagon pinch-bolts in the crown bracket.   Each lower fork-tube cover assembly can now be pulled out from below.   If the tube appears to be tight, open the split of the crown bracket slightly with a taper wedge and replace top plugs, but only screwing down a few threads.   Give the plugs a sharp blow with a mallet and the tubes will slide downwards.   Take off the coil springs, replace and then proceed to fit up in the reverse way to dismantling.

Before fitting the coil springs ensure that they are well packed with thick grease, otherwise there is a tendency for a dry spring to " chatter " against the outer covers.

Dismantling

After very lengthy service or damage, it may be necessary to dismantle completely the fork assembly.

This is best carried out by first removing the whole assembly from the steering head of the frame.   Remove damper knob and column locknut Y (see Fig. 39).   Lift off handlebar bracket and speedometer mounting if fitted.

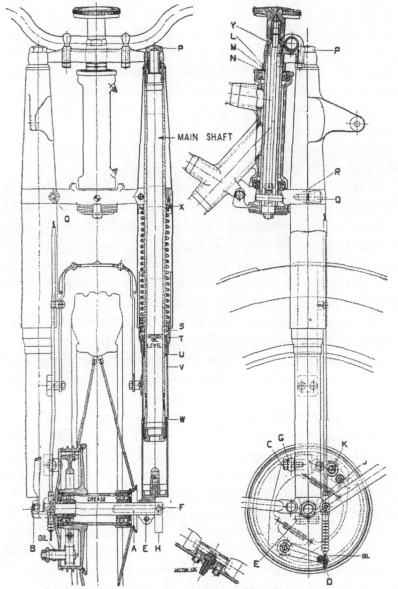

FIG. 39.—THE 1947-51 ARIEL TELESCOPIC FORK WITH HYDRAULIC
CONTROL. THE 1951 SPEEDOMETER MOUNTING IS NOT SHOWN.

Remove other column locknuts L and M and note position of the self-adjusting spring plate which automatically adjusts the steering-head ball races. The steering column and crown carrying the complete fork assembly can now be withdrawn downwards. Take care not to lose the steel balls from the head races.

After removing coil springs as previously described, continue dismantling by unscrewing the sleeve S locating the special oil-seal. A service tube spanner supplied by the makers is essential for this operation.

A stiff wire circlip T securing the top bush U is next removed and whilst holding the main tube in the jaws of a vice, suitably protected with soft clamps, tap gently with a mallet or hide hammer on the end of the sliding tube V and the bottom bush W will drive out the top bush U.

The main fork tube can now be removed complete with the lower bush, which is secured with a sleeve nut.

To remove bottom outer cover, detach the three short screws with a long screwdriver. The top cover can be lifted clear after removing the handlebar bracket, with which is incorporated the speedometer mounting on certain 1950 and on all 1951 models.

The main inner fork-leg tubes are turned from high-tensile manganese-carbon steel, tested to 45 tons/sq. in., and if at all damaged are extremely difficult to reset without special tools and jigs. Therefore, it is advisable always to return a damaged assembly to the makers or to fit new replacement component parts. When reassembling the telescopic fork, ensure that all parts are thoroughly cleansed, especially the white-metal-covered top and bottom bushes, oil-seals, etc. Foreign matter will prevent the sliding and damper action from working effectively.

If the white-metal bushes appear worn or scored these should be replaced and no attempt made to re-metal them. The 1949–51 models are fitted with special bronze bushes which entirely supersede the 1947/8 pattern, but are interchangeable throughout the complete range. The self-adjusting oil-seals, which have, when new, internal diameters of $\frac{1}{16}$ in. less than the outer diameter of the main tubes, should be replaced after very long service.

Reassembly

First replace the outer covers, leaving handlebar bracket and locknuts loose. Slide the oil-seals and the housings S over the main leg tubes and also the top bushes U, Fig. 39. Next insert the bottom bushes W in the sliding tubes V. Secure each main tube between the protected vice jaws and place a split tube or sleeve, which is obtainable from the makers or agents, over the tube so that it makes contact with the end of the vice jaws on one side and the top bush U on the other.

Tap the end of the sliding tube V to force right home the bush U. Refit circlips T and screw up the sleeves S securely. Insert the main tube assembly into the crown and handlebar bracket, loosely tighten the top plugs P and finally tighten the nut Y below the steering damper knob. Tighten plugs P and lastly the two pinch-bolts in the steering crown. Remove plugs P again and refill to correct level with recommended grade of oil.

Head Races

Repack top and bottom head races with grease and refit to frame, taking note of the self-adjusting layout. Between the two column locknuts L and M and the ball-race dust cover, a spring diaphragm N is located. The spring action of this automatically adjusts the head races against wear to a certain degree. After lengthy service, however, clearance may develop in the head races and spanner adjustment is essential.

Support the front of the machine by placing a block

FIG. 40.—DISMANTLING TELESCOPIC FRONT FORK ASSEMBLY—1.
Removing wheel. Offside hub spindle nut has been removed and the set spanner used to loosen fork-end pinch-bolt. The tube spanner finally removes hub spindle.

FIG. 41.—DISMANTLING TELESCOPIC
FRONT FORK ASSEMBLY—2.

Detaching main fork shaft and
lower cover assembly after top plug
has been removed.

FIG. 42.—DISMANTLING TELE-
SCOPIC FRONT FORK—3.

Removing the coil springs.
Solo type can be exchanged for
heavy duty springs for side-car use.

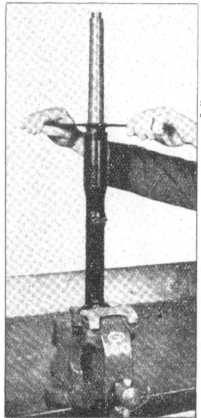

Fig. 43   (*Left*).—Dismantling
Telescopic Front Fork—4.

Removing sleeve and oil-seal with
special service tool to gain access to
circlip retaining top bush.

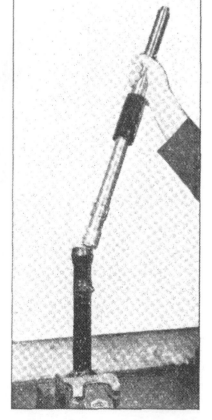

Fig. 44 (*Right*).—Dismantling
Telescopic Front Fork—5.

Lifting out main shaft complete
with lower bush (W on Fig. 39).

under the engine to allow the wheel to clear the ground. Slacken off the top column locknut L and screw down the bottom nut M until all clearance is taken up. Then further tighten the nut one-sixth of a turn. Hold the nut securely and tighten the top locknut L.

Test the steering carefully, and if any roughness is felt, worn or pitted races and steel balls are probably the cause. Instructions regarding replacement of head races will be found in Chapter X.

Steering Damper

The construction of the damper is similar to the type fitted to girder fork models, but in place of the usual middle link spindle location the lower end of the damper rod is secured by a parallel steel peg driven into and through the crown at the base of the steering column. The peg also passes through the brass trunnion piece connected to the end of the rod. To dismantle the complete damper, punch out the parallel peg, unscrew damper knob and remove the small damper plate anchorage bolt and nut. The whole assembly can then be withdrawn. After very lengthy service the friction fabric disc may require renewal, otherwise no replacement should be necessary except in case of damage.

TELESCOPIC FORK ASSEMBLY DATA

Special tools necessary for dismantling and assembling consist of :—

    1. T type tube spanner for sleeve S carrying oil-seal on main tube.
    2. Hexagon socket key for pinch-bolt marked Q.
    3. Split sleeve for main tube and bush assembly.

        (Obtainable from makers and agents.)

Top and bottom white-metalled bushes obtainable only from makers and agents.

Auxiliary Coil Springs.

   Code : " Yellow Spot "   .   .   Solo type.
     Number of coils   .   .   .   20
     Wire gauge .   .   .   .   0·202 in.
   Code : " Red Spot "   .   .   Side-car type.
     Number of coils   .   .   . $19 + \frac{1}{2}$.
     Wire gauge .   .   .   .   0·212 in.

CHAPTER IX

WHEELS, HUBS AND BRAKES

Front Wheel and Brake (except 1947-51 Telescopic Fork Assembly Type)

To take off the front wheel, remove bolt from top end of brake anchor bar. Remove knurled adjusting nut on bottom end of brake rod. Disconnect speedometer cable at lower end if front-wheel driven type. Slacken spindle nuts, pull washers out of recesses in fork ends and wheel can be pulled out complete.

After taking out the wheel, undo the brake plate complete with shoes, and then pull off the shoes. Lightly grease the brake cam spindle, clean and grease the cam spindle bearing so that it will move on the brake plate and centralise the shoes when the brake is applied.

Examine the brake linings and treat as described for the rear wheel.

Removal of front wheel bearings—bearing adjustment and lubrication are as described for the rear wheel.

Reassembly is simply the reversal of the instructions for dismantling, but be sure that the brake plate anchor bar is secure, that the spindle nut washers are properly located in the fork ends, and the spindle nuts are tight.

To adjust the brake, screw up the knurled adjusting nut on the brake rod as far as it will go without the brake rubbing.

Front Wheel and Brake (1947-51 Telescopic Fork Assembly Type)

The construction of the front hub for this assembly only is similar to that of the detachable rear wheel fitted to 1936–1939 models when specially ordered from the makers.

Instead of the taper roller bearings as fitted to the front hub of all previous Ariel models, the 1947/8/9 hub includes two single-row ball journal bearings pressed into the centre shell. Special rubber sealing washers are used to cover the bearings when fitted to prevent ingress of foreign matter.

The front brake is identical with all previous types, except that the adjustment is carried out by means of the fulcrum instead of the usual milled, round adjusting nut on the brake rod.

Maintenance consists only of lubrication of the hub bearings, brake cable and cable nipple. The bearings are not adjustable. No grease nipple is fitted to the hub centre. To lubricate, remove the hub spindle by un-screwing the end nut on the brake side and loosen the pinch-bolt on the offside fork end. The hub spindle can now be withdrawn by using a tommy bar passed through the hole in the spindle end and pulling and twisting the spindle right out. Every 4000–5000 miles insert about a teaspoonful of thin grease into the hub through the spindle hole. Adjustment for brake lining wear is made by turning clockwise the square-headed fulcrum attached to the brake plate. The brake cable stop is adjusted to take up any initial stretch of the cable and should not be used otherwise.

Removal of Hub Ball Bearings

Both bearings are a tight fit in the hub shell and can be removed only by first unscrewing the locking rings on either side, and, with a soft punch tool inserted through the shell and driven up against the abutment at the back of each bearing, driving it out. When fitting new ball journals, which must be pressed or driven in, ensure that care is taken to apply pressure or driving load to the outer race only. Any pressure applied to the centre race will cause undue stress on the actual bearing surfaces and steel balls. When refitting the locking rings and rubber sealing washers to this hub, take care that the ring does not lock up solid the inner race of the bearing, otherwise the driven wheel will force the race to rotate on the spindle and form a groove, with resultant excessive shake and clearance. Note that the brake-side ball bearing is fitted with a centre steel sleeve for spindle reduction. The sleeve and bearing is supplied by the makers of the motor cycle assembled ready for fitting, and riders are advised not to interfere with it.

Rear Wheel and Brake with Fixed Wheel and Rigid Frame (1936–1951, all Models)

To take off the wheel, remove wing nut on brake rod, disconnect chain, uncouple front end of brake anchor bar, slacken spindle nuts, and lift hinged portion of guard and pull out wheel.

To remove the brake, after removing wheel, undo brake plate locknut and remove brake plate complete with shoes and then pull off the shoes. Lightly grease the brake cam spindle, fulcrum adjustment wedge and spindles.

Examine the brake linings for wear and, if necessary, fit new linings or replacement shoes and linings. If new linings are fitted, see that they are riveted down so that they lie in close contact with the shoe. Also see that the rivet heads are countersunk in the lining and that the foot of the rivet is carefully punched over.

Removal of Bearings and Adjustment

First take out the wheel and remove the brake plate as described above.

Screw off the two thin adjusting and locking nuts,

G and H (Fig. 45) and tap out the spindle towards the
brake drum side. Prise off the two dirt-excluding covers;
these will probably be damaged and, therefore, require
replacement. The inner races, rollers and cages of the
taper roller bearings will drop out complete.

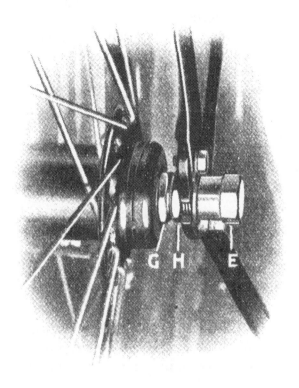

FIG. 45.—WHEEL BEARING ADJUSTMENT.

The outer races are pressed into the hub and should not
be removed needlessly. Each race bears against an abutment washer in the hub tube. Remove the race by driving
out with a drift placed through the hub and bearing up
against the back of the abutment washer.

Examine the track of the outer race. The inner race-
track cannot easily be seen, as it is masked by the rollers

and roller cage.   However, wash in petrol, examine as
well as possible, and also examine the taper rollers and the
cage.   If any parts are seriously worn or damaged replace
the whole bearing assembly, *i.e.*, outer race together with
inner race, rollers and cage.

When the wheel has been refitted to the frame, slacken
the outer spindle nut E on side opposite brake drum ; hold

FIG. 46.—REAR BRAKE ADJUSTMENT.

inner cone adjusting nut G and loosen outer locknut H.
Adjust inner nut, and then, still holding this inner nut,
tighten the locknut and the outer spindle nut.   When the
bearing is correctly adjusted there must be just the slightest
slack as measured at the rim.

Brake Adjustment

All normal brake adjustment must be made by rotating
the square-ended fulcrum screw situated in the brake

plate diametrically opposite the brake lever bearing
(Fig. 46). Turn clockwise to compensate for wear. The
hand adjuster on the rear end of the brake rod must be
slackened off whilst the fulcrum adjustment is made.
When the fulcrum spindle will turn no further, re-tighten
the hand adjusting nut until the brake pedal has only a
trace of idle movement. Always adjust the rear brake by
means of the fulcrum adjuster. The thumbscrew on the
brake rod must only be used to compensate for rear-chain
adjustment. This is important if good braking and even
wear on the brake linings are to be obtained.

The wedge holder, *i.e.*, the part carrying the fulcrum
screw, is riveted to the brake plate on early models but is
bolted to the plate on later machines. Bolts, not studs,
cast-in to the wedge holder, are used. Therefore, do not
try to unscrew the bolts from the holder. Simply unscrew the nuts outside the brake plate and withdraw the
holder. Put shakeproof washers under the nuts when
replacing.

The hub should be packed with grease during assembly
or grease may be pumped in via the grease nipple after the
bearings have been assembled, but before the brake plate
is fitted. Spin the wheel a few times, holding by the
spindle, and wipe off any surplus grease which works out
past the bearings.

Detachable Rear Wheel

A quick detachable rear wheel was first introduced in
1936, fitted to certain models only, and discontinued
during the 1939 season. This type of wheel is carried
on a hollow spindle and has two single-row ball journal
bearings in the hub, and a similar bearing in the brake
drum centre.

The brake drum and sprocket are located on a fixed
spindle bolted to the nearside fork end and construction,

maintenance and lubrication are identical with the drum and brake assembly of the fixed wheel.

One ball bearing of the single-row journal type is fitted to the brake drum—pressed into position with a metal grease-retaining washer either side and finally secured with a flat circlip. The bearing can be removed for replacement purposes by removing circlip and retaining-washer and punching out with an offset tool. When fitting new bearing apply pressure only to the outer race.

The two hub bearings are treated in the same way as the brake type, with the exception that they are finally secured by locknuts and a circlip. Note position of hub-spindle distance collars and fork-end sleeve when reassembling the wheel into the frame.

A detachable rear wheel was again introduced for 1950 models, and this was designed on lines similar to the previous wheel except for details of the layout of the hub spindle and distance pieces. The wheel hub is fitted with only one ball bearing instead of two as previously, and a similar bearing is fitted to the brake drum centre. See " Data " page 165.

Hub bearings of any description, provided with correct lubrication and adjustment where possible, should give a useful service of from 30,000 to 40,000 miles. To determine whether ball journal bearings require replacement, the wheel should be tested for " shake " when fitted to the frame, and rim play should not exceed $\frac{1}{8}$ in.

Taper roller bearings as fitted to non-detachable wheels and being adjustable, do not show " play " so readily, but when wear takes place it usually sets up a roughness through pitting of the rollers and outer race.

Brake Adjustment

Where the Ariel fulcrum adjustment is incorporated, this fitment, being of car design, allows the brake linings to bear more or less evenly over the whole length of the fabric and therefore ensures far longer life than when fitted with the rod or cable control only.

Brake operating cams can be stoned or ground if slightly grooved, but replacement is advisable if badly worn.

Brake drums, if seriously scored, should be replaced, but where the braking surface is not deeply marked, the drum interior can be cleaned up on the lathe and the linings slightly packed with thin shim steel to compensate.

Very thin grease should never be used for hub lubrication, as this has a tendency to work through and saturate brake linings as well as leaving the bearings to dry off frequently.

Notes on Wheel Building

Buckled or dented rims will cause a wheel to run out of true and the complete wheel should be rebuilt if possible. Wheel building is work for the experienced mechanic only and the following points must be closely watched, owing to different makers employing different types of material and design. Ensure correct type of rim as specified by the makers, *i.e.*, width, diameter, quantity of spoke holes and angle of holes.

Ariel rims are usually thirty-six hole front and forty-hole rear, but a check should always be made before ordering replacements. Never attempt to fit a rim of another make, because the allotted spoke angle may not match up with the corresponding flange of the hub.

All Ariel rims are specially prepared with spoke holes at the correct angle and it should be noted that all holes on one side of the rim are of a much more acute angle than the other side. The acute side must be fitted to correspond with the brake drum side of the wheel, otherwise the spokes are liable to " kink " when tensioned.

1937–1951 1000-c.c. and 1939 600-c.c. models are

fitted with the rear portion of the frame offset to the near or left-hand side in order to accommodate the overhung portion of the transmission, and to compensate and position the rear wheel rim centrally in relation to the top frame tube and front rim, the rear wheel is built out of centre and known as " dished ". Any person engaged upon wheel building will understand this term and should be told, therefore, to build the rim over and out of centre to the permissible allowance of $\frac{1}{4}$ in. The rim is " dished " over towards the right-hand or offside. Double diameter or butted spokes are fitted to the brake side of all

FIG. 47.—1950 DETACHABLE REAR WHEEL SHOWN WITH RIGID FRAME AND 1939/1949–50 HINGED-TYPE REAR MUDGUARD.

wheels.   If spoke breakage occurs, it is advisable to replace the complete side or set.   Running a wheel with
broken and missing spokes always imposes severe stress
on the remaining ones and the angle head is generally
somewhat weakened.

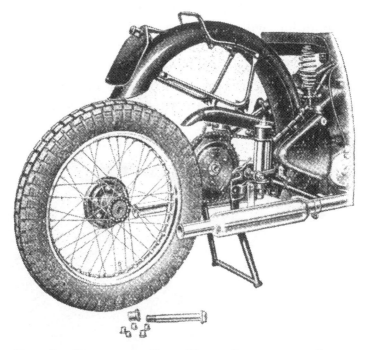

FIG. 48.—DETACHABLE REAR WHEEL SHOWN WITH SPRING
FRAME AND THE 1951-TYPE REAR MUDGUARD AND STAYS.

Always grind away the protruding ends of spokes where
they pass through the nipples and ensure that the rim tape
is fitted to protect the inner tube.

Wheel Alignment

Procure a plain board about 6 ft. long, 3 in. wide and
$\frac{3}{4}$ in. thick ; see that one edge is perfectly straight.   With
the machine on the stand, place the straight edge of the
board alongside the two wheels so that it touches each
wheel.   Turn the handlebars, if necessary, so that the

front wheel touches the edge of the board at two points. If the wheels are in perfect alignment the board will also touch the rear wheel at two points. If it does not touch in this manner, slack off the rear-wheel spindle nuts and turn the chain adjusters until the wheel touches the board at two points. The handlebars may require turning very slightly to adjust the position of the front wheel to correspond with the new position of the rear wheel.

When the two wheels are in proper alignment, the straight edge of the board will touch each wheel at two points.

DATA ON WHEELS, HUBS AND BRAKES

Fixed front and rear wheels with rigid frame.
Hub bearings—Timken taper roller, size $\frac{9}{16}$ in. $\times$ $1\frac{3}{4}$ in. $\times$ $\frac{9}{16}$ in.

Fixed rear wheel with spring frame.
Hub bearings—Single-row ball journal, size 2 in. $\times$ $\frac{3}{4}$ in. $\times$ $\frac{11}{16}$ in. 2 off.

Detachable rear wheel with rigid and spring frame 1936–1939.
Hub bearings—Single-row ball journal, size $\frac{7}{8}$ in. $\times$ 2 in. $\times$ $\frac{9}{16}$ in. 2 off.

Brake drum with detachable wheel 1936–1939.
Drum bearing—Single-row ball journal, size $\frac{7}{8}$ in. $\times$ $2\frac{1}{4}$ in. $\times$ $\frac{11}{16}$ in. 1 off.

Front wheel with telescopic fork 1947–1951.
Hub bearings—Single-row ball journal, size 2 in. $\times$ $\frac{3}{4}$ in. $\times$ $\frac{11}{16}$ in.

Detachable rear wheel, all models 1950–1951.
Hub bearing—Single-row ball journal, size $\frac{3}{4}$ in. $\times$ 2 in. $\times$ $\frac{11}{16}$ in. 1 off.

Brake drum with detachable wheel, all models 1950–1951.
Drum bearing—Single-row ball journal, size $\frac{7}{8}$ in. $\times$ 2 in. $\times$ $\frac{9}{16}$ in. 1 off.

BRAKE LININGS.

1936–1937 . Front, size $5\frac{3}{4}$ in. $\times$ 1 in. $\times$ $\frac{3}{16}$ in.
Rear, size $6\frac{5}{8}$ in. $\times$ 1 in. $\times$ $\frac{3}{16}$ in.

1938–1947/8/9 . Front, size $5\frac{3}{4}$ in. $\times$ $1\frac{1}{8}$ in. $\times$ $\frac{3}{16}$ in. (girder fork) ; $6\frac{5}{8}$in. $\times$ $1\frac{1}{8}$ in. $\times$ $\frac{3}{16}$ in. (1947–1951 telescopic fork).
Rear, size $6\frac{5}{8}$ in. $\times$ $1\frac{1}{4}$ in. $\times$ $\frac{3}{16}$ in.

1939 250-c.c. only . Front, size $5\frac{3}{4}$ in. $\times$ $\frac{7}{8}$ in. $\times$ $\frac{3}{16}$ in.
Rear, size $6\frac{5}{8}$ in. $\times$ $1\frac{1}{8}$ in. $\times$ $\frac{3}{16}$ in.

SPOKES.

    Plain type   .   .   No. 10 gauge.
    Butted type .   .   No. 10 gauge butted by No. 8 gauge.

RIMS AND TYRE SIZES.

    WM1 .   .   .   20 for 3·00 in. × 20 in. tyre.
    WM2 .   .   .   19 for 3·25 in. × 19 in. tyre.
    WM3 .   .   .   18 for 4·00 in. × 18 in. tyre.

The 3·00 × 20 front tyre is fitted to a $2\frac{1}{4}$ × 20 rim. The most suitable oversize is 3·25 × 20.

The 3·25 × 19 tyres are fitted to $2\frac{1}{2}$ × 19 rims and oversizes are 3·50 × 19 and 4·00 × 19, although the latter is better mounted on a 3 × 19 rim. The 4·00 × 18 tyre is fitted to a 3 × 18 rim and this is the largest available tyre.

TYRE PRESSURE.

Actual tyre pressures are dependent upon several factors, such as load carried, normal running speed and road conditions, etc. For average use the following are the recommended minimum inflation pressures for Dunlop cord tyres, given in lb. per sq. in. :—

	Tyre Size.	Front.	Rear.	Side-car.
Solo . .	3·00 × 20	26	—	—
	3·25 × 19	20	26	—
	3·50 × 19	16	22	—
	4·00 × 18	16	18	—
Side-car .	3·00 × 20	30	—	—
	3·25 × 19	22	32	16
	3·50 × 19	18	26	16
	4·00 × 18	16	20	16

If a pillion rider is carried, the rear tyre pressure should be increased to carry the extra load.

CHAPTER X

RIGID AND SPRING FRAMES

Rigid Frame

APART from occasional lubrication of the steering-head bearings and the general tightening of all bolts, studs and nuts, no maintenance or repairs are necessary. In the case of a frame being damaged by accident, the average motor cyclist is advised to send it to the makers for repair. Special building jigs and fixtures are necessary to ensure that the frame is in perfect alignment, and the makers, with full knowledge of the type of tubing incorporated, can best determine when and where heat should be applied for the final setting process.

When the forks have been removed the top and bottom head races should be closely examined for any signs of pitting.

Head Races

These races or caps are hardened and ground and are a tight press- or driving-fit in the frame-head lug. Pitted or worn cups should be replaced, because perfect steering depends upon the condition and adjustment of the head races and steel balls. It is advisable to replace the balls if suspected at any time of being chipped or worn. The races or cups can be removed from the head lug by driving out from opposite ends, using an offset punch or drift long enough to pass through the length of the lug. New races can be inserted by press action or, if a press is not available, place a hard-wood block on the race and drive them in squarely.

Spring Frame

The rear spring frame attachment, or in reality the rear spring wheel, was introduced in 1939 and when incorporated into a complete frame can be fitted to all Ariel models from 1936 and subsequent with the exception of the 1939 250-c.c. lightweight model. Existing standard rigid frames cannot be converted to sprung type without completely rebuilding the whole of the rear half of the frame, but the makers do not undertake this conversion and can only supply, in normal times, a complete frame with the attachment.

Keep the assembly well lubricated and all working parts will give exceptionally long service. Replacements are not necessary for at least 40,000-50,000 miles. Ensure that the stirrup arm H is adjusted by means of screwing up the square-headed bolt G after loosening the locknut (see Fig. 49). Do not over-tighten or the sliding action will be suppressed. Keep the connecting-link bolts tight.

Wear in the link-spindle bushes and stirrup-arm bushes after long service is remedied only by replacements.

Chain Adjustment

1936-1949 *Models.*—Adjustment is carried out by independent operation of the separate cams fitted against the rear fork ends of the stirrup arms " H ". (See Fig. 49.)

1950-1951 *Models.*—The stirrup arms " H " are fitted with adjuster bolts " P " and lock nuts " Q ", and adjustment is similar to that for wheels fitted to rigid-type frames. (See Fig. 50.)

Dismantling Spring Frame Attachment

This is best carried out by removing the rear wheel; support the machine by placing a suitable block or box under the engine.

Remove the dome nut under the assembly which screws on to the end of the centre bolt K. Pull out centre bolt K and top collar N. This collar is not threaded. The remainder of the centre assembly, consisting of the main coil spring, the slider B, the guide tube A, collar D, dust tubes L and M, bottom recoil spring and the thick base packing piece, can all be lifted out quite simply.

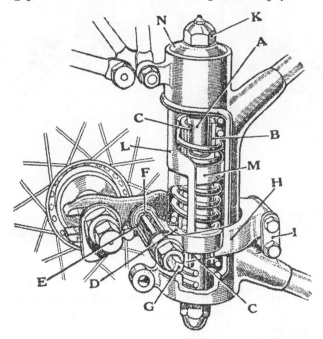

Fig. 49.—Section of Spring Wheel Arrangement (1939–1948/9).

Remove the pivot pin G from the wheel side of the stirrup and take out link spindles and links I.

Thoroughly examine the slider bushes C and renew if showing wear when tested on the guide tube A and spindle K. The bushes are a press-fit and should be reamed after fitting to correct size. See frame data on p. 171. Also test the pivot-arm bush E on spindle G and renew if worn. This bush is also a press-fit.

The connecting-link spindle bushes are of the graphite

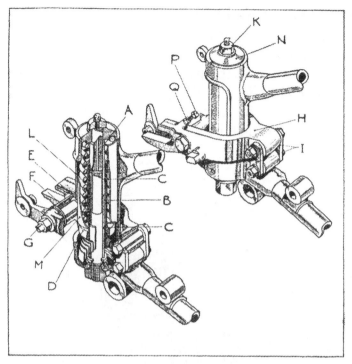

FIG. 50.——SECTION OF REAR SPRING WHEEL ATTACHMENT,
1950–1951.

compounded self-lubricating type, but should be tested
for ovality wear and pressed out for renewal if necessary.

Reassembly

Fit the dust-excluding tube L into the main cylinder
from the top with the cut-away portion facing backwards.
Next place in position the thick base packing-piece and
the short, flat section recoil spring.   Next place in position
the slider B, locating same with the short extension below
the collar D.   Above the collar fit the dust tube M and
the main coil compression spring.   Assemble the top
collar N on to bolt K, followed with the guide tube A,
and pass this sub-assembly down through the slider B
until the end of bolt K projects through the base of the

main cylindrical lug.   Screw on the bottom dome nut and thoroughly tighten.   In order to save unnecessary work with the grease-gun, it is a good plan to pack well with grease the interior assembly before fitting into position.

If the spring attachment appears to " bottom " whilst the machine is being used on rough roads, it is a sign of main coil-spring weakness.   Stronger springs are fitted to the Square Four model and can also be incorporated in the attachment of any single-cylinder machine if desired.

The centre stand originally fitted to early 1939 spring-frame models was subsequently superseded by a rear spring-up type stand.   A special conversion set, incorporating the stand and adaptable brackets, can usually be obtained from the makers.

The head lug and ball races of the spring frame are identical with those of the rigid type and the same maintenance and service treatise therefore applies.   A damaged frame should always be returned to the makers for repair and correct alignment.

DATA ON FRAMES

Spring Frame.

Sliding member bush (4 off).   Ream after fitting to

$$\left.\begin{array}{l} 0 \cdot 8745 \text{ in.} \\ 0 \cdot 8755 \text{ in.} \end{array}\right\} \text{diameter.}$$

Stirrup arm bush (4 off).   Ream after fitting to

$$\left.\begin{array}{l} 0 \cdot 625 \text{ in.} \\ 0 \cdot 6245 \text{ in.} \end{array}\right\} \text{diameter.}$$

Connecting-link bolt bush (4 off).   Ream after fitting to

$$\left.\begin{array}{l} 0 \cdot 625 \text{ in.} \\ 0 \cdot 6245 \text{ in.} \end{array}\right\} \text{diameter.}$$

Main spring top 0·296 in. diameter wire " VH " and " 4F " 600-c.c.

Main spring top 0·312 in. diameter wire " 4G " 1000-c.c.

FRAME INTERCHANGEABILITY (RIGID AND SPRING)

RIGID FRAME.

The single-cylinder rigid frame is interchangeable with every model 500-c.c., 350-c.c. and 250-c.c. produced in 1936 and subsequent, excepting the 1939 250-c.c. lightweight models. All engine and gearbox fixing plates, frame bolts, etc., are likewise identical.

SPRING FRAME (SINGLE-CYLINDER).

The spring frame, first manufactured in 1939, can be fitted to all models produced since 1936, excepting the 1939 lightweight 250-c.c.   Engine plates, etc., are identical.

SPRING FRAME (FOUR-CYLINDER).

The spring frame (four-cylinder type) can be fitted only to the 1937–1951 Square Four 1000-c.c. and the 1939 four-cylinder 600-c.c.   Engine plates, etc., are identical.

CHAPTER XI

THE RED HUNTER MODELS "VH" AND "NH" FOR COMPETITION USE

ARIEL MOTORS have never manufactured for general release any form of a special racing machine, and the factory supported riders up to the 1949 season always confined their competitive efforts to the use of standard single-cylinder 350-c.c. and 500-c.c. Red Hunter models suitably geared for any type of reliability trial or sporting scramble entered.

A post-war " British Experts Trial " was won by an Ariel rider using a Model " VH " geared to conform to the conditions of the day.

The Hunter lends itself to tuning for competition use, and such as reliability trials and scrambles, and the really small amount of work necessary can be carried out by the average keen sports rider.

The works do not supply any special racing quick-lift cam assemblies or special engine components of any description, although certain other agencies claim to have produced good samples of such fitments.

Generally, therefore, it can be taken that the standard Hunter model, as delivered from the factory, has been designed to produce the highest all-round performance for all general purposes, whilst with very slight modifications, a first-class trials mount can be evolved.

The compression ratios obtained with Ariel L.C. and H.C. pistons are low for racing with special fuels, but for trials purposes are very satisfactory when used with a 50/50 petrol benzol mixture. The H.C. gives a compression ratio of 7·5 : 1, and this is considered ideal for straight events and high-speed scrambles.

Many riders make the mistake of using too high gear ratios. Hunter models are fitted with standard Burman gearboxes and rear-wheel sprockets. A range of engine driving sprockets should be obtained and used on the trial and error system to ascertain which ratio is suitable for a given course. The Experts' Trial course of cross-country and muddy lanes necessitated a 19-T. engine sprocket with the "VH" model and a 17-T. with "NH" models. Reference should be made to the data at the end of Chapter VI for various ratios obtainable by exchanging engine sprockets.

General Tuning—Engine

To ensure against loss of power by friction, it is essential to remove the cylinder barrel several times during the " running in " stages, and carefully examine the piston for high spots, denoted by highly polished portions over the bearing faces.

These so-called " spots " should be gently removed by filing with the finest of pocket files and polishing.

Time spent on the piston is well worth while and frictional losses can be reduced to a minimum.

Rings should be quite free in the grooves and well " gapped " to ensure against any tendency for the ends to meet or " butt ".

The gudgeon-pin bush can be reamed to give an extra 0·0005 in.–0·001 in. clearance to the pin.

The head can be super-polished without altering the contours of the valve ports, etc., and this work again will be well rewarded. Grind in the head to the top of the barrel, and check the threads of all holding bolts.

Valve stems can be highly burnished and the bore of

the guides lapped and polished. An extra 0·001 in. clearance is permissible here.

Face or surface finish is an asset to all bearing surfaces, and light polishing of cams, cam levers and rockers all tends to reduce friction.

Flywheels and connecting-rod are polished steel on Hunter models and no further attention is called for. With the dry sump lubrication system, very little " oil drag " can be associated with the flywheel assembly and crankcase interior, and therefore these parts should remain standard.

The connecting-rod should be checked for alignment, and be in perfect relationship to the cylinder bore. Any mal-alignment of the rod will be in evidence and shown up by high witness marks on one face or side of the piston.

Carburetter

The joint flange must match up very accurately with that of the cylinder-head induction port, and both faces should be rubbed down on a flat surface plate.

Trial and error tests should be made with various jet and throttle-valve settings, but do not tune too seriously to obtain full maximum power output and sacrifice low-down regular pulling, which is essential to have at times in many reliability trials.

Ignition

If a B.T.H. or Lucas competition magneto can be obtained this should be fitted in place of the magdyno.

Dynamos and headlamps are not a necessity for trials purposes, providing one has the means of transportation to and from the trials venue. Whichever unit is used, magneto or magdyno, care should be taken to render it as waterproof as possible. A liberal supply of plasticine should be smeared over the H.T. pick-up and cable connection, and round the edge of the contact-breaker cover after ensuring that the contact screw is correctly set and tightened.

Endeavour to tune the engine with the maximum advance of $\frac{5}{8}$ in. B.T.D.C. if possible.

The most suitable plug is dependent on the type of fuel used, but for 50/50 petrol benzol and the high-compression ratio of 7·5, a Lodge HNP, or makers' equivalent, is suitable for short-distance trials, and a cooler running type such as a Lodge R49 for long-distance events and when maximum power output has to be maintained for lengthy periods.

An excellent plug is now being marketed by the K.L.G. people and bears a code prefix letter " W " which denotes " Waterproof ". The K.L.G. W.F70, is a good general-purpose plug, but many makers' alternatives appear from time to time, and agents' lists should be consulted regarding these.

Lubrication, Control Cables, Gearbox

No modification is necessary to the standard dry sump system, and providing absolute cleanliness is adhered to when preparing for trials, no trouble should occur. For short-distance events, a thin grade of oil can be used to advantage, but frequent flushing of the sump and oil-tank should be carried out between events.

Check and adjust all controls in order to obtain full range of movement. An excellent plan of precaution, in case of control failure during an event, is to have a complete spare set of cables made up and taped in position with those in use, just leaving the ends ready for quick attachment if any particular cable fails.

A very light grease or grease-and-oil mixture can be used for the gearbox and will assist with gear changing, especially during very cold weather conditions (see also page 121). If fabric insert clutch-plates are used, ensure that stronger clutch springs are also incorporated to prevent slip.

Cycle Parts, Silencers, Steering

Both wheels must be checked for bearing adjustment and be perfectly free, brakes efficient, but not binding. Chain lines should be checked over in relation to their respective sprockets.

Silencers should be thoroughly cleaned internally to eliminate any tendency for back pressure to occur.

Steering-head adjustment should be such as to allow perfect freedom without slackness in the bearings. With the telescopic fork assembly, a heavier grade of oil is permissible for cross-country trials and scrambles and has a tendency to reduce fork bounce or bottoming.

COMPETITION MODEL "VCH" 500 c.c. 1949/51

A very limited number of special competition models coded under the heading "VCH" were first produced for the 1949 season.

The basic design and lay-out of the machine is almost identical with that of the Model "VH", except that a light-alloy cylinder barrel and head are fitted to light-alloy crankcases.

A short-wheel-base high-ground clearance frame is used with a standard telescope-fork assembly. A lighting set is not fitted, ignition being by Lucas or B.T.H. competition magneto.

For home use and very suitable for scrambles and trials purposes a Burman wide-ratio "CP" type gearbox is fitted, whilst for export a "BA" close-ratio unit is incorporated.

All data relative to maintenance and adjustments of the

standard model " VH " are applicable to this model
" VCH " (see technical data following).

Data Table

Engine :

    Bore, 81·8 mm.
    Stroke, 95 mm.
    Compression Ratio, 6·8–1 with standard piston.
    B.H.P. at 6000 r.p.m., 25.

Gear Ratio :

    " CP " Gearbox—Wide Ratio—19T. Engine Sprocket
    (2-Plate " Neoprene " fabric compound Clutch). 1st
    Gear, 19·1 to 1.   2nd Gear, 12·6 to 1.   3rd Gear, 9·16 to 1.
    Top Gear, 6·05 to 1.

    " BA " Gearbox—Close Ratio—19T. Engine Sprocket
    (3-Plate " Neoprene " Clutch). 1st Gear, 15·3 to 1.
    2nd Gear, 9·7 to 1.   3rd Gear, 7·2 to 1. Top Gear,
    5·75 to 1.

    " BA " Gearbox—Close Ratio—21T. Engine Sprocket
    (3-Plate " Neoprene " Clutch). 1st Gear, 13·9 to 1.
    2nd Gear, 8·8 to 1.   3rd Gear, 6·5 to 1. Top Gear,
    5·15 to 1.

CHAPTER XII

ELECTRICAL EQUIPMENT

THE Lucas magdyno has been fitted to nearly all Ariel motor cycles since 1931. Up to and including 1936 the single-cylinder magdyno, with the ring cam type contact breaker and the three-brush non-voltage-control dynamo, was fitted. In 1937 the Lucas face type cam contact breaker was introduced for single-cylinder models, together with the automatic voltage control type dynamo (2-brush). The single-cylinder magneto drive of the well-known " slipping clutch " type was first introduced in 1937 and is still being fitted to all units.

All 1932–1948 four-cylinder models are fitted with the early ring cam contact breaker and fixed gear drive. The slipping clutch drive cannot be adapted to this type magdyno.

Four-cylinder type dynamos are of the A.V.C. type and have been fitted to all 1000-c.c. models and the 1939 600-c.c.

The 1948–51 twin-cylinder models are fitted with either Lucas or B.T.H. magnetos and separate Lucas dynamos. Both magnetos are fitted with the ring cam and pivot rocker arm type contact breaker.

The 1949–51 1000-c.c. models are fitted with Lucas dynamo and coil ignition system (see Technical Data at end of Chapter).

Lubrication

The magdyno driving gears and housing are packed with H.M.P. (high melting point) grease when the unit is

new and this is sufficient for at least 20,000 miles' service.
A small quantity of grease can, however, be inserted into
the gear housing after withdrawing the dynamo. Armature bearings are also well packed with lubricant when
new and only require further attention during the annual
or other time overhaul depending on conditions and mileage.

The contact-breaker cam of the ring type is lubricated
by a short piece of felt located in the ring housing. In a
small hole of the cam ring is fitted a small wick which

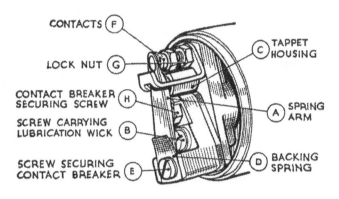

FIG. 51.—THE FACE CAM TYPE OF CONTACT BREAKER.

absorbs oil from the felt and keeps a minute film of lubricant on the face of the cam ring.

Every 5000 miles withdraw the ring and soak the felt
with several drops of thin machine oil. Having removed
the contact breaker to gain access to the ring, it is advisable
to lubricate the breaker-arm pivot bearing. Turn aside
the locating spring and prise the rocker arm off its pivot
and smear a small quantity of vaseline petroleum jelly on
the bearing.

The face cam type is lubricated by a wick contained in
a screw behind the moving contact spring blade. Remove
the blade and wick screw and thoroughly soak wick in oil.
At the same time pull out the hard fibre composition
tappet which operates the moving blade and lightly smear

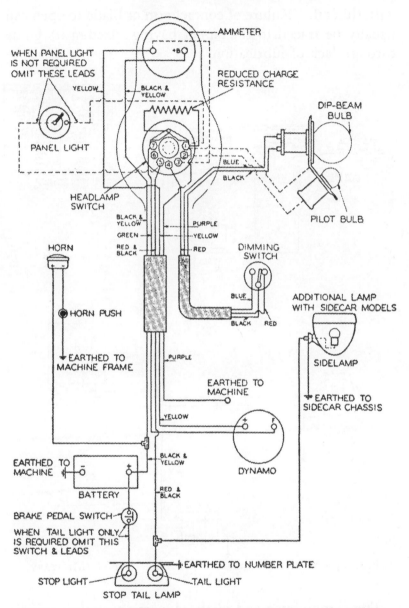

WHEN PANEL LIGHT
IS NOT REQUIRED
OMIT THESE LEADS

AMMETER

+B

REDUCED CHARGE
RESISTANCE

YELLOW

BLACK &
YELLOW

DIP-BEAM
BULB

PANEL LIGHT

7

6   5

1   2

4   3

BLUE

BLACK

HEADLAMP
SWITCH

PILOT BULB

HORN

BLACK &
YELLOW

PURPLE

GREEN

YELLOW

RED &
BLACK

RED

DIMMING
SWITCH

HORN PUSH

BLUE

BLACK   RED

ADDITIONAL LAMP
WITH SIDECAR MODELS

EARTHED TO
MACHINE FRAME

PURPLE

SIDELAMP

EARTHED TO
MACHINE

EARTHED TO
SIDECAR CHASSIS

YELLOW

EARTHED TO
MACHINE

BLACK &
YELLOW

DYNAMO

BATTERY

RED &
BLACK

BRAKE PEDAL SWITCH

WHEN TAIL LIGHT ONLY
IS REQUIRED OMIT THIS
SWITCH & LEADS

EARTHED TO NUMBER PLATE

STOP LIGHT

TAIL LIGHT

STOP TAIL LAMP

FIG. 52.—WIRING DIAGRAM FOR LUCAS MAGDYNO LIGHTING
EQUIPMENT AS FITTED TO ARIEL MOTOR CYCLES, 1933–1936.

with thin oil. Failure of contact arm or blade to open can usually be traced to the tappet having seized in its guide through lack of lubrication.

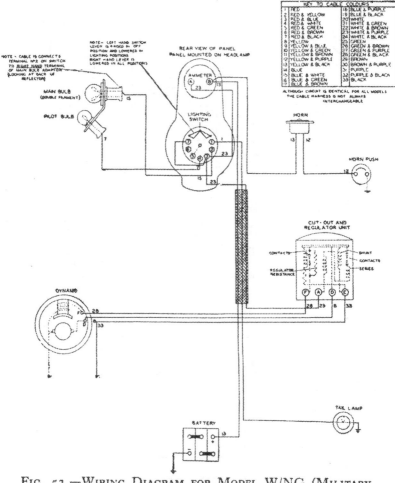

FIG. 53.—WIRING DIAGRAM FOR MODEL W/NG (MILITARY, X/WD).

The commutator end of the dynamo armature spindle runs in a plain bush or bearing surrounded by a felt ring. To lubricate the bearing the felt must be kept soaked in thin machine oil, inserted by way of the ball valve in the dynamo end-cover. Several drops of oil should be forced in every 2000 miles to ensure good service of this bearing. As with the magneto portion, the main dynamo ball bearings are packed with grease when new and subsequently at each annual or other periodic overhaul.

Adjustments

Contact breakers should be examined for correct setting of contact points at least every 2000 miles or at any time if difficult starting or poor performance is experienced.

Rotate the engine until the contacts are fully opened and insert the feeler gauge attached to the magneto spanner (0·012 in. thick) between the two points. Loosen the contact screw locknut and adjust the screw until the gauge just slides between the points and re-tighten locknut. If the breaker points have been subjected to long service, renewals are advisable. A contact set, consisting of

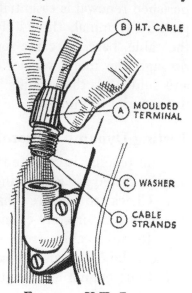

FIG. 54.—H.T. PICK-UP ASSEMBLY.

adjustable screw and rocker arm for ring cam type or screw and spring blade for face type, can be obtained from the makers and agents. Points can, however, be cleaned and refaced squarely by using a very fine magneto file or carborundum stone.

When replacing the contact breaker of the ring cam type, be sure to see that the projecting keyed portion engages with the keyway cut in end of the armature spindle. Do not over-tighten the centre hexagon-headed securing pin.

The H.T. pick-up should be periodically removed and the carbon brush and spring examined and wiped with petrol.   See that the brush and spring are free to slide in the holder.

With the pick-up removed, clean the armature slip-ring surface and track by inserting a clean cloth and pressing on the ring whilst the engine is slowly rotated by hand.

Examine the pick-up holder carefully for any signs of "tracking" or cracks and if the H.T. lead or cable is perished renewal is essential.   To fit the new cable to the pick-up terminal, thread the knurled moulded nut over the cable, bare the cable for about $\frac{1}{4}$ in., thread the wire through the metal washer removed from the old cable and fold back the strands.   Finally, screw the moulded nut into its terminal.

Testing Dynamo (Automatic Voltage Control Type)

If no reading is obtained on the ammeter, the dynamo may be tested for generating as follows :

1. Check to ensure that the dynamo and A.V.C. regulator are correctly connected (see Fig. 55).

2. Remove cables from dyno terminals D and F and connect the terminals with a short length of cable wire.

3. Start engine and set to run at a low throttle idling speed.

4. Connect the positive lead of an ordinary moving-coil voltmeter (zero–10 volts type) to one of the dynamo terminals and connect the negative lead to any clean bare earthing-point on the dynamo body or engine.

5. Gently increase the engine speed and the voltmeter reading should rise without fluctuation.   If no reading is indicated, do not rev. engine to obtain a reading, but check the brush assembly.   If only a low reading is registered of, say, $\frac{1}{2}$ volt, the field winding may be defective, whereas if a reading of $1\frac{1}{2}$–2 volts is obtained, the

armature winding may be at fault. Never allow the voltmeter reading to exceed 12 volts.

6. To examine armature commutator and brush

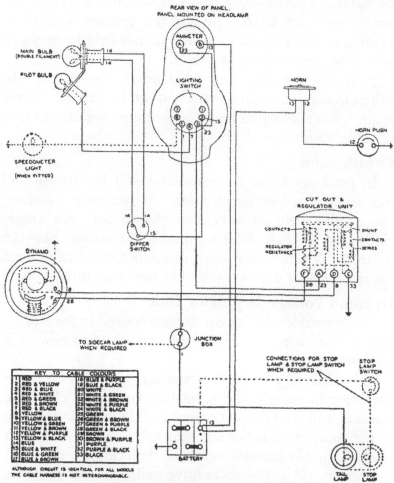

FIG. 55.—LUCAS MAGDYNO COMPENSATED VOLTAGE CONTROL EQUIPMENT AS FITTED TO ARIEL MOTOR CYCLES, 1937–50, EXCEPT TO THE 1949–1950 1000-C.C. MODELS WITH COIL IGNITION.

assembly, remove the cover band. Pull back the brush springs and ensure that the carbon brushes are free in the guides by pulling gently on the flexible connections. If brushes are slow in action or sticking in their guides, remove them and polish lightly with a smooth file or fine emery cloth. Worn brushes that do not bear on the commutator should be replaced. Clean the commutator by holding a petrol-soaked cloth against it and turn engine over slowly by hand. Re-test the dynamo and if no reading is obtained the complete unit should be replaced with a new or serviced armature.

7. If the dynamo is in good order, connect up the cables in correct original order and test by running engine again. No reading on ammeter will now indicate a break in cable leads.

Commutator

In good condition a commutator will be smooth and free from pitted or burnt spots. If requiring attention, use a thin strip of very fine glass-paper—not emery cloth—and polish whilst rotating armature between centres. A very badly worn commutator indicates need for replacement with a serviced or new armature.

Dynamo Voltage Regulator Unit

The regulator and the cut-out are housed in the A.V.C. unit and are correctly set by the makers when new or if serviced later.

Only after very long periods of service will it be found necessary to remove the protecting cover and clean the contacts, and even this operation should not be undertaken if the unit is functioning correctly. Messrs. Joseph Lucas Ltd., the manufacturers of the complete electrical equipment, advise owners to leave well alone and when the unit requires attention to return it to them or one of their depots for exchange or servicing.

Plugs

Detachable plugs should be dismantled and cleaned with a wire brush and petrol, and the electrodes set to give a gap of 0·015 in.–0·018 in.

ELECTRICAL SERVICE NOTES AND TEST DATA
Ariel 498-c.c. KG 1948/50, and KH 1949/51 Twins

The electrical equipment, unless otherwise stated, is the *Lucas 6 volt with negative earth return.*

Dynamo.—Lucas 20009A. Two-pole ventilated design; compensated voltage control; clockwise rotation viewed from driving end.

Crossed connections will cause serious damage to the regulator. Connect lead with *yellow identity tag* to main terminal, and *green-and-black tracer cable* to field terminal.

Test Data.—Dynamo cold: Cutting-in speed 1200–1400 r.p.m. at 7·0 dynamo volts. Output 5·0 amps. at 1800–2000 r.p.m. at 7·0 dynamo volts, taken on 1·4-ohm resistance load without regulator. (Resistance must be able to carry 7·5 amps. without overheating.) Brush tension 10–15 oz. Field resistance 3·1–3·3 ohms.

Magneto.—Lucas K2F AC53, and B.T.H.—KC2 Form W4 (LM).

Anti-clockwise rotation viewed from driving end.

Contact-breaker gap 0·012 in.–0·015 in.

Condenser capacity 0·1–0·14 microfarad.

Test Data.—Centrifugal advance commences at 620–720 r.p.m. and gives maximum advance of 15°–18° at 1075 r.p.m.

Control Box.—Lucas MCR L-2. Houses cut-out and dynamo voltage regulator.

Test Data.—(*a*) Cut-out. Cut-in voltage 6·3–6·7 volts; drop-off voltage 4·5–5·0 volts.

(*b*) Regulator. Setting at 10° C. (50° F.) 7·8–8·2 volts; setting at 20° C. (68° F.) 7·8–8·2 volts; setting at 30° C. (86° F.) 7·7–8·15 volts; setting at 40° C. (104° F.) 7·6–8·1 volts.

Headlamp.—Correct lamp settings are important to prevent dazzle.

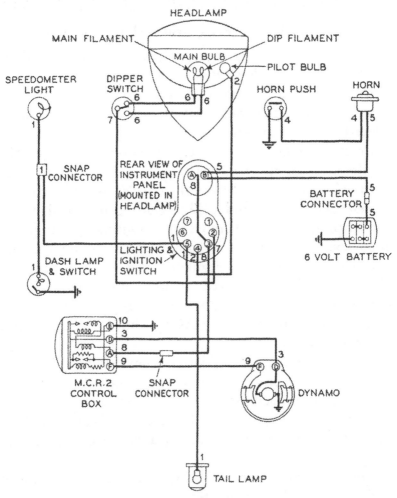

KEY TO CABLE COLOURS

1 RED		6 BLUE
2 RED & BLACK		7 BLUE & WHITE
3 YELLOW		8 WHITE & PURPLE
4 YELLOW & PURPLE		9 GREEN
5 YELLOW & BLACK		10 BLACK

FIG. 56.—WIRING DIAGRAM ARIEL 500-C.C. TWIN-CYLINDER
MODELS KG AND KH, 1948–49 (NOT 1950).

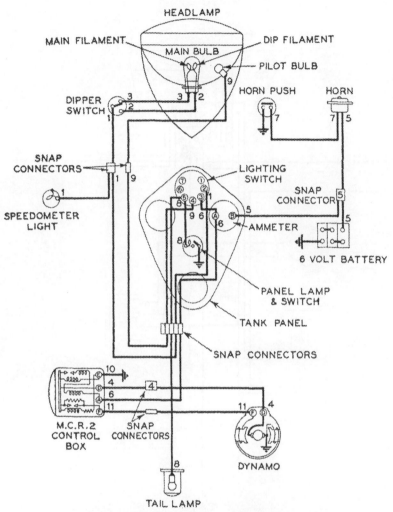

KEY TO CABLE COLOURS

1 BLUE		7 BROWN WITH BLACK
2 BLUE WITH RED		8 RED
3 BLUE WITH WHITE		9 RED WITH BLACK
4 YELLOW		10 BLACK
5 BROWN		11 BLACK WITH GREEN
6 BROWN WITH WHITE		

FIG. 57.—WIRING DIAGRAM ARIEL 500-C.C. TWIN-CYLINDER
MODELS KG AND KH, 1950.

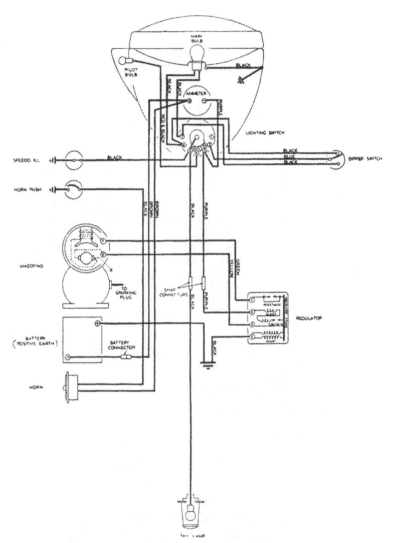

FIG. 58.—WIRING DIAGRAM ARIEL SINGLE-CYLINDER
MODELS 1951.

The diagram for the twin-cylinder model is similar except that the
magneto and dynamo are separate and the magneto supplies two
plugs.

Horn.—High-frequency type. Current consumption 4 amps. (approximate).

Battery.—Capacity 12 amp. hour, at 10 hour rate.

The importance of carefully carrying out the initial charging of the battery cannot be overstressed, as in the early stages of its life it can be completely ruined by non-adherence to the following charging instructions :

Carefully break seals in filling holes and half-fill each cell with dilute sulphuric acid, specific gravity 1·270. The battery should be allowed to stand at least 6 hours before further electrolyte is added.

Allow to stand a further 2 hours before commencing charge.

Initial charge rate 0·8 amp. for approximately 50 hours.

Correct electrolyte to 1·280–1·300 at completion of charge when voltage and specific gravity remain constant.

The figures given are for Home Trades and climates ordinarily below 80° F. (27° C.).

For sub-tropical climates between 80° and 100° F. (27° and 38° C.) the appropriate figures are : Filling, 1·245 ; Fully charged, 1·250–1·270.

For tropical climates over 100° F. (38° C.) the figures are : Filling, 1·220 ; Fully charged, 1·220–1·240.

For complete charging instructions, see Lucas Publication No. 732A. Recharge at 1·5 amps.

Battery should be topped-up to the level of separators, using distilled water only.

Battery terminals should be kept clean, and connectors tight.

Ariel 4G, 1000-c.c., Models 1949/51

The electrical equipment, unless otherwise stated, is the *Lucas 6 volt with positive earth return.*

Dynamo.—Lucas 22003B. Two-pole ventilated design; compensated voltage control; clockwise rotation viewed from driving end.

Crossed connections will cause damage to the regulator. Connect lead with *yellow identity tag* to main terminal, and *green-and-black tracer cable* to field terminal.

Test Data.—Dynamo cold: Cutting-in speed 1000–1150 r.p.m. at 6·5 dynamo volts. Output 10·0 amps. at 1700–1850 r.p.m. at 7·0 dynamo volts, taken on 0·7-ohm resistance load without regulator. (Resistance must be able to carry 15 amps. without overheating.) Brush tension 16–18 oz. Field resistance 2·6–2·8 ohms.

Distributor.—Anti-clockwise rotation viewed from driving end.

Contact-breaker gap 0·010 in.–0·012 in.

Contact-breaker spring tension 20–24 oz. measured at contacts.

Condenser capacity 0·2 microfarad.

Test Data.—Centrifugal advance commences at 200–350 r.p.m. (distributor) and gives maximum advance of 21°–23° at 2300 r.p.m.

Ignition Coil.—Current consumption: 1·6 amps. (approximate) running; 3·5–4·0 amps. (approximate) stall.

Coil moulding must be kept clean.

Control Box.—See 498-c.c. model.

Headlamp.—Correct lamp settings are important to prevent dazzle.

Horn.—See 498-c.c. model.

Battery.—See 498-c.c. model, except certain series of 1951 models 1000-c.c. which are fitted with larger capacity 20 amp. hour type.

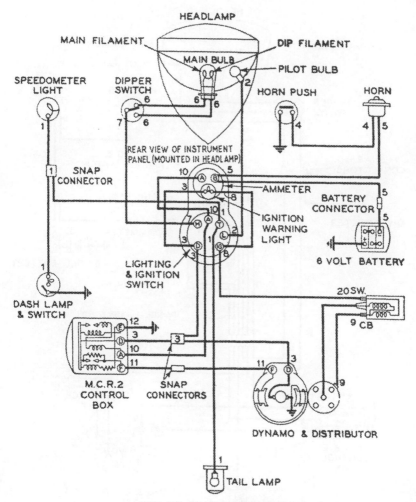

FIG. 59.—WIRING DIAGRAM ARIEL 1000-C.C. SQUARE FOUR, 1949 AND 1951 (NOT 1950).

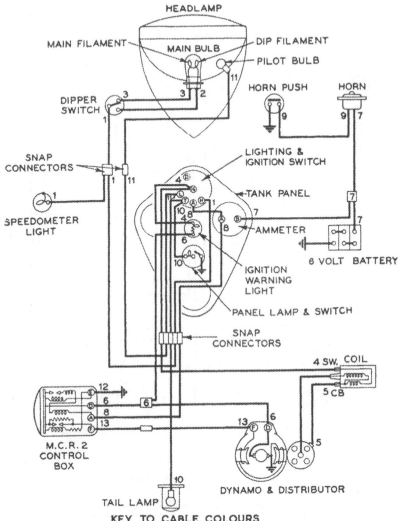

KEY TO CABLE COLOURS

1 BLUE	6 YELLOW	11 RED WITH BLACK
2 BLUE WITH RED	7 BROWN	12 BLACK
3 BLUE WITH WHITE	8 BROWN WITH WHITE	13 BLACK WITH GREEN
4 WHITE	9 BROWN WITH BLACK	
5 WHITE WITH BLACK	10 RED	

FIG. 60.—WIRING DIAGRAM ARIEL 1000-C.C. SQUARE FOUR, 1950 MODELS ONLY (COIL IGNITION).

Ariel NG 347, VG 497, NH 3-47, VH 497, VB 600, Single-Cylinder Models 1937–1951

The equipment is the *Lucas 6 volt with negative earth return* excepting 1951 models with positive earth return.

Dynamo.—Lucas 200285. Two-pole ventilated design; compensated voltage control; clockwise rotation viewed from driving end.

Crossed connections will cause serious damage to the regulator. Connect lead with *yellow identity tag* to main terminal and *green-and-black tracer cable* to field terminal.

Test Data.—Dynamo cold : Cutting-in speed 1200–1400 r.p.m. at 7·0 dynamo volts. Output 5·0 amps. at 1800–2000 r.p.m. at 7·0 dynamo volts, taken on 1·4 ohms resistance load without regulator. (Resistance must be able to carry 7·5 amps. without overheating.) Brush tension 10–15 oz. Field resistance 3·1–3·3 ohms.

Magneto.—Anti-clockwise rotation viewed from driving end.

Contact-breaker gap 0·010 in.–0·012 in.

Condenser capacity 0·13–0·15 microfarad.

Control Box.—The data the same as on 498-c.c. model.

Headlamp.—Correct lamp settings are important to prevent dazzle.

Horn.—See 498-c.c. model.

Battery.—See 498-c.c. model.

APPENDIX

LUBRICATION RECOMMENDATIONS

ENGINE, 4 CYL., IN SUMMER : Castrol " XXL " ; Essolube 50 ; Motorine " B " de Luxe ; Triple Shell ; Mobiloil " BB ". WINTER : Castrol " XL " ; Essolube 30 ; Motorine " E " ; Single Shell ; Mobiloil " A ".

ENGINE, SINGLE CYL., IN SUMMER : Castrol " Grand Prix " ; Essolube 50 ; Motorine " B " de Luxe ; Triple Shell, Mobiloil " D ". WINTER : Castrol " XXL " ; Essolube 40 ; Motorine " C " ; Double Shell ; Mobiloil " BB ".

ENGINE, TWIN CYL., IN SUMMER : Triple Shell ; Mobiloil " BB " ; Castrol " XXL " ; Essolube 50 ; Energol S.A.E. 40. WINTER : Double Shell ; Mobiloil " A " ; Castrol " XL " ; Essolube 40 ; Energol S.A.E. 30.

GEARBOX : Castrolease Medium ; Esso Grease ; Belmoline " C " ; Shell Retinax " CD " ; Mobilgrease No. 2.

OIL-BATH CHAINCASE AND REAR CHAIN : Engine oil.

WHEEL HUBS : Castrolease Heavy ; Esso Grease ; Belmoline " C " ; Shell Retinax " RB " ; Mobil Hub Grease.

GENERAL GREASING : Castrolease " CL " ; Esso Grease ; Belmoline " C " ; Shell Retinax " CD " ; Mobilgrease No. 2.

TELESCOPIC FORKS—NORMAL CONDITIONS : Castrol " XL " ; Essolube 30 ; Motorine " C " ; Double Shell ; Mobiloil " A ". ARCTIC CONDITIONS : Castrolite ; Essolube 20 ; Motorine " E " ; Single Shell ; Mobiloil Arctic.

The use of any good proprietary brand of running-in compound containing Acheson colloidal graphite is recommended for running-in a reconditioned or new engine. The compound should be added to the engine oil in the proportion of one pint per gallon for the first few thousand miles, after which reduce to half a pint per gallon, following on at a quarter of a pint for general use.

Upper-cylinder lubricant containing colloidal graphite added to the fuel can be used to advantage throughout the life of an engine. Instructions for use of the latter are given on the makers' containers.

INDEX

AMAL carburetter, 129

Bearings
  armature, 180
  big-end, 13, 30, 31, 37, 95, 111
  brake drum, 161
  camshaft, 13, 33, 38, 99, 110
  crankcase, 32, 101, 104, 111
  crankcase oil seal, 25
  crankshaft, 11, 13, 30
  driving gear, 121, 128
  mainshaft, 128
  steering head, 139, 167
  wheel, 156, 157
Big-end
  bearings, 13, 30, 31, 37, 95, 111
  oil-feed hole, 32
  side float, 96
Bi-starter carburetter, 15, 136
Brake
  adjustment, 155, 159, 161
  data, 165
  drum, 160
  linings, 155, 157, 165
  removal, 155, 157
Breather valves, 88

Cam
  contact-breaker, 179, 183
  gear, 99, 100, 101, 112
Camshaft
  bearings, 13, 33, 38, 99, 110
  chain, 13
  sprocket, removing, 29
Carburetter
  Amal, 129
  body fixing flange, 134
  data, 133
  maintenance, 129
  Solex, 15, 135
  tuning, 175
Chain
  driving, 128
  timing, 88
Chain wheel, clutch, 118, 127
Clutch
  assembly, 113
  cable adjuster, 114
  cork, 125
  data, 127
  dismantling, 115
  fabric, 125

Commutator, 186
Competition models, VH, NH and VCH, 173–178
Compression rings, gap, 13
Connecting-rod, 30, 31
  alignment, 75
  bearings, 13, 30, 31, 37, 52, 95, 111
  side float, 96
Contact breaker, 179, 183
  gap, 12
Coupling gears, crankshaft, 27
Crank assembly, dismantling, 11
Crankcase
  bearing oil seal, 25
  bearings, 32, 101, 104, 111
  condensation in, 9
  dismantling, 25, 101
  filter, 15
  inspecting, 32
  oil level, 12
  reassembling, 33, 105
Crankpin
  fitting to flywheels, 104
  parallel, 104
  taper, 102, 104
Crankshaft
  assembly, 27, 28, 49, 76
  bearings, 11, 13, 30
  coupling gears, 27
  dismantling, 25
  gear assembly, removing, 10
  reassembly, 33, 77
  sprocket, removing, 29
Cylinder
  assembly, 91
  bore, 37, 72
  bore wear, 23, 72
  head gaskets, 22
  refitting, 23, 69, 96
  removal, 17, 23, 51, 67, 91

Damper
  fork, adjusting, 139
  steering, dismantling, 143
  steering, telescopic fork, 153
Decarbonisation, 10, 17, 44, 67, 90
Distributor
  gear, removing, 35
  timing, 35
Driving-gear
  bearings, 121, 128
  bushes, 120

Driving-side
  mainshafts, testing, 104
  threads, 104
Dynamo
  testing, 184
  voltage regulator unit, 186

Electrical equipment, 179
Electrical service notes and test
    data
  four-cylinder, 192
  single-cylinder, 195
  twin-cylinder, 187
End-play, mainshaft, 123
Engine
  plates, refitting rear, 106
  removal, 70, 97
  replacing, in frame, 107
Engine data
  4F/600, 1933–6, 12–14
  4F/600, 1939, 36–38
  4G/1000, 1937–48, 36–38
  4G/1000, 1949 onwards, 56
  single-cylinder, 109–112
  twin-cylinder, 81
  VCH, 178
Engines
  4F/600, 1933–6, 9–14
  4F/600, 1939, 15–38
  4G/1000, 15–38
  4G/1000, light-alloy, 39–58
  competition models, VH, NH and
    VCH, 173–178
  single-cylinder, 83–112
  twin-cylinder, 59–82
Exhaust-valve lifter, adjusting, 89

Filter
  crankcase, 15
  oil-tank, 85
  sump, 85
Flange
  carburetter body fixing, 134
  magneto sprocket hole, 32
Float chamber, 134
Flooding, carburetter, 134
Flywheels, 104
  alignment of, 105
  assembly, dismantling, 102
  refitting, 105
Foot
  gear-change mechanism, 113, 123
  rest rod distance piece, 107
  rests, removing, 25
Fork, front
  dismantling, 142, 146
  girder type, 138
  leg tubes, main inner, 148
  main springs, 144, 145

Fork, front (contd.)
  spindle bushes, 143
  spindles, 138, 143, 144
  telescopic, 145
Four-cylinder engines, 9–58
Frame
  data, 171
  rigid, 167
  spring, 168
  spring, data, 171
Front
  brake, 155
  forks, girder type, 138
  forks, telescopic, 145
  wheel removal, 155
Fulcrum screw, brake, 156, 159

Gaskets, cylinder-head, 22
Gauge, oil-pressure, 85
Gear
  change mechanism, foot, 113, 123
  crankshaft coupling, 27
  pinions, 120
  ratios, 127
  timing, reassembling, 106
  timing, removing, 29
Gearbox
  assembly, 113
  data, 127
  dismantling, 115
  lubrication, 121, 176
  reassembly, 122
Girder type front fork, 138
  data, 144
  repairing, 144
Gudgeon pin
  bush, 174
  clearance, 92
  diameter, 13, 37, 111
  removing, 24
Guides, valve and tappet, 90

H.T.
  leads, 36
  pick-up assembly, 183, 184
Handlebar mounting, 141
Hub data, 165

Ignition
  system for competition use, 175
  timing, 12, 34, 107, 110

Jet
  air correction, 136
  block, 133
  main, 132
  needle, 132, 134

KG and KH twin models, 59–92

Kick-starter
lever return spring, 124
quadrant, 119, 124

Layshaft spindle bush, 122
Lifter, exhaust-valve, adjusting, 89
Light-alloy engine, 4G, 39–58
Links, fork, 145
Lubrication
armature bearings, 180, 182
contact-breaker, 180
engine, 9, 16, 41, 60, 84, 86, 108
front forks, 141
gearbox, 121, 176
recommendations, 196

Magdyno, 179
chain, 14, 88
removal, 29, 74, 98
sprocket hole flange, 32
sprocket, removing, 29
Magneto, fitting, 79, 106
Magneto timing, 80
Main jet, 132
Mainshaft,
bearings, 128
end nut, removing, 115
end-play, 123
testing, 104

Needle
float, 134
jet, 132, 134
throttle, 132

Oil
breather valves, 88
consumption, excessive, 86
control rings gap, 13
feed hole, big-end, 32
feed pipe, 106
feed, testing, 86
filter, 9
level, crankcase, 12
pressure, 11, 13, 41, 60, 63
pressure gauge, 85
pressure valve, 17, 41
pump ball valve, 11, 17, 86
pump data, 110
pump, dismantling, 15, 42
purifier, 84
return pipe, 88
return, testing, 86
seal, crankshaft bearing, 25
seal, gearbox, 121
seals, telescopic fork, 149
tank filter, 85
tank, refilling, 88

Pilot air screw, 129
Pin, cam lever, 101, 112
Pinion, timing, refitting, 106
Pinions, gear, 120
Pipe
oil-feed, 106
oil-return, 88
Piston
clearance, 13, 37, 110
H.C.. compression ratio of, 173
removal, 23, 91
tuning, 174
wear, 23
Piston-rings, 92
gap, 13, 37
Plates, refitting rear engine, 106
Pressure regulator, adjustable oil, 85
Pump
oil, 15, 60, 63, 87, 110
plungers, sliding block, 17
Purifier, oil, 84
Push-rod, clutch, 118
Push-rods, 94

Rear brake
adjustment, 159, 161
removal, 157
Rear wheel
detachable, 160
fixed, 157
spring, 168
Red Hunter models, VH, NH and VCH, 173–178
Red Hunter, tuning, for competition use, 173
Rigid frame, 167
data, 172
Rims, wheel, 163, 166
Rocker
box, reassembling, 22
box, removing, 19, 22, 93, 94
internal bore of, 112
spindle diameter, 112
spindles, removing, 10
Rod distance piece, 100t-rest, 107

Shock-absorber
assembly, 25, 49, 73, 107
dismantling, 25
Silencers, 177
Single-cylinder engines, 83–112
Sliding block pump plungers, 17
Slow running adjustment, 129, 135
Small-end bushes, 24, 37, 92, 111
Solex carburetter, 15, 135
Sparking-plug point gap, 13, 38
Speedometer drive, 125
Speedometers, 126
Spindles, fork, 138, 143, 144

Spokes, wheel, 162, 166
Spring
  diaphragm, telescopic fork, 149
  frame data, 171
  frame, dismantling, 168
  frame, reassembling, 170
  kick-starter lever return, 124
Springs
  coil, telescopic fork, 146
  main, front fork, 144, 145
Sprocket
  camshaft, 29, 61
  crankshaft, 29
  driving gear, 120
  extractor, magdyno, 99
  magneto, 29, 106
  rear wheel, 160
Steering
  assembly data, 144, 153
  damper for girder-type forks, 143
  damper for telescopic forks, 153
  head adjustment for competition
    use, 177
  head assembly, 138
  head bearings, 139, 167
  head dismantling, 142
Sump filter, 85

Tank, oil, refilling, 88
Tappet
  adjustment, 64, 89
  diameter, 112
  guide, internal bore, 112
  guides, 90
Telescopic fork, 145
  data, 153
  dismantling, 146
  reassembling, 149
Tensioner, timing chain, 42, 49, 65
Throttle
  needle, 132
  stop screw, 129
  valve, 129, 137
Timing
  chain, 65, 74, 88
  chain fibre rubber strip, 32
  distributor, 35

Timing (contd.)
  gear removal, 29, 49, 74, 98
  gears, reassembling, 106
  ignition, 12, 34, 54, 80, 107, 110
  pinion, refitting, 106
  side bearings, 29
  side mainshafts, 104
  valve, 12, 33, 54, 78, 109
Top overhaul, 10, 44, 90
Twin-cylinder models, KG and KH,
    59–82
Tyre
  pressure, 166
  sizes, 166

Valve
  ball, oil pump, 11, 17, 86
  breather, oil, 88
  clearance, 12, 37
  exhaust, lifter, adjusting, 89
  guide, internal diameter, 13, 111
  guides, 22, 90
  oil-pressure, 17
  seatings, 21, 90
  spring cotters, removal, 10
  spring removal, 21
  stem clearance, 37, 89, 91
  stem diameter, 13, 111
  throttle, 93, 129, 137
  timing, 12, 33, 54, 78, 109
Valves
  examining, 21
  removal of, 65, 66, 90
Voltage regulator unit, dynamo, 186

Weller tensioner blade, 29, 32
Wheel
  alignment, 164
  bearings, 156, 157
  building, 162
  data, 165
  rear, detachable, 160
  rear, fixed, 157
  rear, spring, 168
  spokes, 162, 166
Wiring circuits, 181, 182, 185, 188,
    189, 190, 193, 194

OTHER CLASSIC MOTORCYCLE MANUALS CURRENTLY AVAILABLE IN THIS SERIES:

ARIEL WORKSHOP MANUAL 1933-1951

A comprehensive manual for all models built between 1933 and 1951. *Four cylinder:* 4/F/600cc OHC, 4/F/600cc OHV, 4/G/1,000cc OHV (Cast Iron & Light Alloy). *Twin cylinder:* 500cc OHV models KG & KH. *Single cylinder:* 600cc SV model VB. 500cc OHV models VG & VH. 350cc OHV models NH & NG. 250cc OHV models OH, OG, LG & LH. Much of the data is applicable to later models that utilize these same engines.

ISBN: 1-58850-071-3

BMW FACTORY WORKSHOP MANUAL R50, R50S, R60, R69S

A reproduction of the factory workshop manual for the R50, R50S, R60, R69S twin cylinder series of BMW's. Also included is a supplement for the USA models: R50US, R60US, R69US.

The text and illustration captions are printed in English, German, French and Spanish and while the translations may at times be a little quirky, the data is comprehensive and invaluable to the BMW enthusiast.

ISBN: 1-58850-067-5

BMW FACTORY WORKSHOP MANUAL R27, R28

A reproduction of the factory workshop manual for the R27 and R28 single cylinder series of BMW's, while quite scarce in the USA these were very popular models in Europe.

The text and illustration captions are printed in English, German, French and Spanish and while the translations may at times be a little quirky, the data is comprehensive and invaluable to the BMW enthusiast.

ISBN: 1-58850-068-3

NORTON FACTORY TWIN CYLINDER WORKSHOP MANUAL 1957-1970

A reproduction of the factory workshop manual for both the *Lightweight Twins:* 250cc Jubilee, 350cc Navigator and 400cc Electra and the *Heavyweight Twins:* Model 77, 88, 88SS, 99, 99SS, Sports Special, Manxman, Mercury, Atlas, G15, P11, N15, Ranger (P11A) which makes this manual appropriate for all Norton models that utilized this series of 500, 600, 650 and 750cc engines through the 1970 model year.

ISBN: 1-58850-069-1

NORTON MAINTENANCE & REPAIR MANUAL 1932-1939

All Pre-War SV, OHV and OHC models: 16H, 16I, 18, 19, 20, 50, 55, ES2, CJ, CSI, International models 30 & 40. Much of the data is applicable to both earlier and later models that utilize the following single cylinder engines: 490cc SV, 633cc SV, 348cc OHV, 490cc OHV, 596cc OHV, 348cc OHC, 490cc OHC. **ISBN: 1-58850-070-5**

TRIUMPH 1935-1939 MAINTENANCE & REPAIR MANUAL

All Pre-War single & twin cylinder models: L2/1, 2/1, 2/5, 3/1, 3/2, 3/5, 5/1, 5/2, 5/3, 5/4, 5/5, 5/10, 6/1, Tiger 70, Tiger 80, Tiger 90, 2H, Tiger 70C, 3S, 3H, Tiger 80C, 5H, Tiger 90C, 6S, 2HC, 3SC, 5T Speed Twin, 5S and T100 Tiger 100.

Much of the data is applicable to earlier models that utilize the following engines: *Single Cylinder:* 250cc OHV, 350cc SV, 350cc OHV, 500cc SV, 500cc OHV, 550cc SV and 600cc SV. *Twin Cylinder:* 500cc OHV and 650cc OHV. **ISBN: 1-58850-066-7**

TRIUMPH 1937-1951 WORKSHOP MANUAL (A. St. J. Masters)

The most comprehensive Workshop Manual available for pre swing-arm Triumph motorcycles. Covers rigid frame and sprung hub single cylinder SV & OHV and twin cylinder OHV pre-war, military, and post-war models: 2H, Tiger 70, Tiger 70C, 3S, 3H, Tiger 80, Tiger 80C, 5H, Tiger 90, Tiger 90C, 6S, 2HC, 3SC, 5T Speed Twin, 5S, T100 Tiger 100, 3HW, 3SW, 5SW, 3T, Grand Prix, TR5 Trophy and 6T Thunderbird.

Much of the data is applicable to earlier models that utilize the following engines: *Single Cylinder:* 250cc OHV, 350cc SV, 350cc OHV, 500cc SV, 500cc OHV and 600cc SV. *Twin Cylinder:* 350cc OHV, 500cc OHV and 650cc OHV. **ISBN: 1-58850-064-0**

TRIUMPH 1945-1955 FACTORY WORKSHOP MANUAL NO.11

The most comprehensive Workshop Manual available for pre-unit, twin-cylinder Triumph motorcycles. Covers the full line of rigid frame, sprung hub, swing-arm and 350cc models: 5T Speed Twin, T100 Tiger 100, TR5 Trophy, 6T Thunderbird, T110 Tiger 110 and 3T De-Luxe.

Much of the data is applicable to later models that utilize the following engines: Twin Cylinder 350cc OHV, 500cc OHV and 650cc OHV. **ISBN: 1-58850-065-9**

VINCENT WORKSHOP MANUAL 1935-1955

Complete technical data, service and maintenance information, and comprehensive detailed instructions for the repair and overhaul of all major and minor mechanical and electrical components for all models of Vincent motorcycles from 1935 through 1955. Also includes a detailed electrical section and a comprehensive chapter on modifications for racing.

ISBN: 1-58850-072-1

PLEASE CHECK OUR WEBSITE OR CONTACT YOUR DEALER
FOR AVAILABILITY
~ WWW.VELOCEPRESS.COM ~

OTHER CLASSIC MOTORCYCLE MANUALS COMING SOON IN THIS SAME SERIES:

ARIEL MAINTENANCE & REPAIR MANUAL 1932-1939
LF3, LF4, LG, NF3, NF4, NG, OG, VA, VA3, VA4, VB, VF3, VF4, VG, Red Hunter LH, NH, OH, VH & Square Four 4F, 4G, 4H. This particular manual has a very good section dealing with the 1933 to 1936 four cylinder OHC engine and required reading if you own one of these rare motorcycles.

BRIDGESTONE FACTORY WORKSHOP MANUAL
50 Sport, 60 Sport, 90 De Luxe, 90 Trail, 90 Mountain, 90 Sport, 175 Dual Twin & Hurricane

DUCATI OHC FACTORY WORKSHOP MANUAL
160 Junior Monza, 250 Monza, 250 GT, 250 Mark 3, 250 Mach 1, 250 SCR & 350 Sebring

HONDA FACTORY WORKSHOP MANUAL
250 & 305cc C.72 C.77 CS.72, CS.77, CB.72, CB.77 [HAWK]

HONDA FACTORY WORKSHOP MANUAL
125 & 150cc C.92, CS.92, CB.92, C.95 & CA.95

HONDA FACTORY WORKSHOP MANUAL
50cc ~ 100, 110, C.100 & C.110

HONDA MAINTENANCE & REPAIR MANUAL 1960-1964
50cc ~ C.100, C.102, C.110 & C.114
125cc C.92 & CB.92 – 250cc C.72 & CB.72

INDIAN PARTS CATALOG ~ 50cc MINI BIKES
A fully illustrated parts manual for the 69 series mini bikes, absolutely
essential information for anyone that owns, maintains, repairs, or is in the
process of restoring a Ponybike, Boy Racer or Papoose.

SUZUKI FACTORY WORKSHOP MANUAL 250/200cc
T10, T20 [X-6 Hustler] T200 [X-5 Invader & Sting Ray]

VESPA MAINTENANCE & REPAIR MANUAL 1946-1959
All 125cc & 150cc models including 42/L2 & Gran Sport

VILLIERS ENGINE WORKSHOP MANUAL
All Villiers engines and ancillaries through 1947

BRITISH MILITARY MAINTENANCE & REPAIR MANUAL
Service & Repair data for all British WD motorcycles

BRITISH MOTORCYCLE ENGINES
AJS, Ariel, BSA, Excelsior, JAP, Norton, Royal Enfield, Rudge, Scott,
Sunbeam, Triumph, Velocette, Villiers & Vincent ~ a compilation of 1950's
articles from *The Motor Cycle* dealing with engine design.

PLEASE CHECK OUR WEBSITE OR CONTACT YOUR DEALER
FOR AVAILABILITY
~ WWW.VELOCEPRESS.COM ~